Gerhard Heufler, Michael Lanz, Martin Prettenthaler

DESIGN BASICS

FROM IDEAS TO PRODUCTS

niggli

Conception: Michael Lanz, Martin Prettenthaler
Authors: Gerhard Heufler, Michael Lanz, Martin Prettenthaler, Ursula Tischner (page 32),
Matthias Götz (pages 88–97), Petrus Gartler (pages 144–146), Gerald Steiner (pages 228–235)
Design: Martin Prettenthaler
Proofreading: Nele Kröger

The Deutsche Nationalbibliothek lists this publication in the Deutsche Nationalbibliografie;
detailed bibliographic data are available on the Internet at http://dnb.dnb.de

 © 2004 Niggli, imprint of Braun Publishing AG, Salenstein, www.niggli.ch
2nd edition 2020, ISBN 978-3-7212-0988-4

Although the male form was chosen in the text for reasons of legibility, the information refers
to members of both sexes. All personal statements are to be understood as gender-neutral.
In particular, "designer" means both the male and female designer.
For better reading, the term "FH JOANNEUM, University of Applied Sciences, Industrial Design,
Graz/Austria" is abbreviated as "FH JOANNEUM Industrial Design" or "FH JOANNEUM".

In continuation and commemoration of the work of Gerhard Heufler, we dedicate this book to the outstanding industrial designer who played a major role in setting up the Industrial Design course. Gerhard Heufler taught at FH JOANNEUM for many years and passed on his theoretical and practical knowledge to many students. His recognized standard work "Design Basics" was revised in the 5th edition by Michael Lanz and Martin Prettenthaler and expanded by new case studies from the FH JOANNEUM Industrial Design Graz.

CONTENTS

Foreword

We live in times of permanent, ever faster changes. This change also affects design and the associated processes. Designers today not only design products, but also entire product systems, possibly even including the associated business models. In addition to economic aspects, ecological and social factors also play an increasingly important role. Design cannot only help to improve the quality of life of consumers through better products, but also to make our society as a whole more sustainable. But this expanded understanding of design, as described by Ursula Tischner in the publication "Was ist EcoDesign?"[1] published by the German Environment Agency or by Bernd Sommer and Harald Welzer in their book "Transformationsdesign"[2], is not as new as many think: as early as 1971 Victor Papanek demanded in his book "Design for the real world"[3] that designers must also assume social responsibility.

In the 1970's, we experienced the oil crisis, today, we experience climate change and the scarcity of resources that increasingly cause designers headaches, which is why many of them are wondering how their work can help solve the many global problems. And that's a good thing, because designers with their distinctive problem-solving skills and their ability to think holistically have particularly good prerequisites for solving such complex tasks.
The fact that design and the associated processes can achieve far more than the design of products or product systems is demonstrated by the design thinking method, which is becoming increasingly popular in many branches of industry. Design thinking draws on user-oriented approaches from the design sector to produce innovative products and services that are geared to the conscious and unconscious needs of users and their abilities. Here it is particularly evident that the usual iterative approach in design can also be successfully applied in other contexts.

The awareness that designers are ideally suited to accompany and actively shape the transformation of companies, NGOs, and even our society as a whole has led, among other things, to the fact that large international management consultancies such as McKinsey, Accenture, Capgemini, to name a few, have begun in recent years to integrate design agencies into their corporate structures.
Talking about the transformation of industry and society, another topic comes to mind: increasing digitalization. Keywords that are closely related to this topic, such as artificial intelligence, the Internet of Things, robotics or big data, are well known in the media. But very few people have a concrete idea of what lies behind it in detail or how these technologies could change the lives of all of us. This ignorance potentially fuels fear and rejection. Here, too, design can help by reducing the "perceived" complexity of these technologies through user-oriented design and making them more comprehensible and accessible for the general public.

The industry has recognized the increasing importance of design for corporate success in many areas. Design has finally become a "matter for the boss", as designers have been demanding for a long time, and so we can already find some top management personalities who have not completed any training in economics or engineering, but have completed a degree in design. While at the beginning of the millennium many companies were still striving to reduce or outsource design departments in order to save costs, a contrary trend has been observed in recent years: the in-house design departments are growing again. Especially in the area of user experience design (UX), specialists are in high demand nowadays. At the latest since the success of the Apple brand, (almost) every product manufacturer today knows about the importance of UX, i.e., a positive experience when dealing with a product, system or service, is for the success of a company.

At the Industrial Design course at FH JOANNEUM in Graz, we are also adapting to the changing requirements of design in the training of future designers. Courses such as "Mechatronics" in which prototyping with Arduino is taught and tested, or "Interface Design and Usability", in which operating concepts for complex applications such as ticket vending machines are developed, take account of the increasing digitalization of the product world. The specializations "Eco-innovative Design" and "Mobility Design" offered in the master program since 2016 also represent a further development. The former deals with the question of how products and product systems can be made more sustainable. It is not only about the use of environmentally friendly materials, but above all about making our lives more sustainable by using products more responsibly, e.g., through intelligent rental systems (keyword "use instead of own") or by changing our lifestyle to be more resource-friendly, socially compatible and thus more sustainable overall. The "Mobility Design" specialization pursues the same goals, but with a focus on mobility concepts. In both areas of specialization, it is therefore becoming increasingly important not only to think in terms of products and product systems, but also to develop the associated services. A designer today no longer thinks in terms of individual solutions, but designs entire product ecosystems and – if it makes sense – supplies the new business model as well.

Some of the design studies shown in this book already reflect the changing role of designers and we are very excited to see what answers the coming generations of Industrial Design students at FH JOANNEUM will give to the challenges of our future.

Michael Lanz
Graz, 2019

List of sources:

(1) Tischner, Ursula et al.: Was ist EcoDesign? Birkhäuser Verlag, Basel, 2000
(2) Sommer, Bernd and Welzer, Harald: Transformationsdesign, oekom Verlag, Munich, 2014
(3) Papanek, Victor: Design for the real world, Thames & Hudson, 2nd revised edition, 1985

How does design develop and what is Industrial Design?

Introduction

History of design

The beginning of the history of design as a scientific discipline is usually associated with the industrial revolution, i.e., the middle of the 19th century. However, the origins go back much further and can be found in related disciplines such as art history, archaeology and architectural history. Since design always has to do with people, the history of design cannot be seen only as a chronology of inanimate things. Rather, it is influenced by other fields of knowledge such as cultural and media studies, philosophy, psychology and linguistics. At the beginning of the 20th century, the training as a designer manifested itself and with it the influence of important thinkers, groups and schools. With the beginning of modernism, the history of design experienced its first climax and parallel to industrial mass production, a functional objectivity developed. The central idea of this period was the sentence "Form follows function", coined by the American architect Louis Sullivan (1856–1924), which became decisive in product design and architecture.[1]

Only with the incipient critique of functionalism in the 1970s did the way become clear for postmodernism as a fundamental counter-movement or extension to modernism. The answer was plurality and more diversity in the individual design directions, ranging from sustainable design to digital design to "art meets design".

Of all the epochs in the history of design, the short period of the Bauhaus idea has so far been most thoroughly researched and documented in scientific publications. Companies in the context of design with historical traditions such as Thonet, Olivetti, Vitra, etc. are simultaneously endeavoring to sketch out their own historical image. A growing number of design museums and their design collections as well as current exhibitions provide a permanent engagement with the research field of design history with their contributions. In addition to the groups mentioned, monographs of works by design authors also exert influence on the young field of research in the history of design.

As standard works on the history of design, we would like to refer to the following authors, amongst others: Catharina Berents (2011), Bernhard E. Bürdek (2015), Petra Eisele (2014), Thomas Hauffe (2014), Victor Margolins (2016), Gert Selle (2007)

From agrarian society to industrial revolution

Design is as old as human history!

Since man has been using tools, the question immediately arises as to how these tools should be designed. Already in the primeval times of human development a certain material was brought into form for a certain function. For example, the hand wedge was one of the first man-made products. In this early phase of agrarian society, everyone made the tools for their own use. Here the producer and consumer are still identical, and each manufactured product is unique in its own way, i.e., a unicum.

Objects with appeal long before the industrial revolution

Royal carriage from Tutankhamun
Ancient design for a monarch who ruled from 1332 to 1323 BC

Already more than 3,000 years ago, a royal carriage of high artistic quality was produced in the Egyptian high culture. The discovery of the tomb of Pharaoh Tutankhamun (18th dynasty) allows us to witness these art treasures. These objects have a very high symbolic appeal. A quality that has become increasingly important in recent design history with the advent of postmodernism. The ceremonial carriage of the Pharaoh probably served less for hunting or duels than for representative purposes. These objects were produced only for the monarchical ruler and not for a broad mass. Nevertheless, the craftsmen and artists had to have a high level of expertise, which we still admire today.

Of course, all these artefacts (objects of craftsmanship) are not objects of designers, but are assigned to craftsmanship, archaeology or the history of art and architecture. Nevertheless, these products are witnesses of past advanced civilizations that produced tools, vehicles, war equipment, etc. and of course had to deal with questions of design. The origins of a pronounced product culture and thus of design go back to antiquity.

Tutankhamun ascended the throne in Egypt in 1332 BC as king of the 18th dynasty. The carriage with a high symbolic charisma was probably used as a state carriage (replica).

Vitruvius and first design theoretical approaches

Leornardo da Vinci
A polymath in the Renaissance period, 15th and 16th century

On our journey through time we will remain in ancient times and would like to refer to the Roman architect, engineer and theorist Vitruvius (ca. 80–10 BC) and his "Ten Books on Architecture". In the third chapter of the first book the following guiding principle is formulated: "All buildings must satisfy three categories: strength (firmitas), suitability (utilitas) and beauty (venustas)."[2]

"Vitruvius thus basically created the basis for a concept of functionalism that came into effect in the 20th century and determined modernity in design."[2] This is a first design theoretical approach that closely relates the usability and beauty of products.

We continue our journey through time and stop at Leonardo da Vinci (1452–1519) in the Renaissance, the transition from the Middle Ages to modern times. In terms of the working process, this polymath can be called the first designer because he knew how to reconcile intellectual intention and artistic freedom. His investigations into the ideal proportions (Vitruvian Man) as well as the precise anatomical drawings and construction plans of flying machines reflect precisely these abilities. Leonardo da Vinci is regarded as an ingenious inventor, designer, master builder, scientist – and ultimately also as a talented designer.[3]

Leonardo da Vinci, The Vitruvian Man proportion drawing, ca. 1492

Self-portrait Leonardo da Vinci, ca. 1515, red chalk drawing 33.2 x 21.2 cm

Technical inventions at the beginning of the industrial age

Preindustrial design – historicism – industrial revolution
Inventions – social upheavals – euphoria and technology, 19th century

Fundamental technical inventions and social change shaped the 19th century. In Europe there was a sharp increase in the population. The number of inhabitants more than doubled, from 180 million (around 1800) to 460 million (1914), resulting in growing demand for products. In the field of medicine, the first vaccines and the X-ray method were developed. Chemistry was on the advance and the production of aluminum and chlorine proved to be successful. So we are talking about the beginning of the industrial age, in which the first products were mass-produced on an industrial scale. Thomas Alva Edison invented the light bulb, Isaac Merritt Singer the sewing machine and Carl Benz built the world's first automobile. These inventions were dominated by experiment and construction. The question of design receded into the background and often lacked historical models.

In the development of the design, different epochs were stylistically influential. The diagram below provides an overview of the various periods and their temporal extent. Not all epochs have a clear beginning and a precise end, the transitions are often fluid. In some styles, such as organic design, the influence reaches back to our time. On the following pages the most important epochs are presented with influential representatives.

Overview of time diagrams of important design epochs in the 19th and 20th centuries:

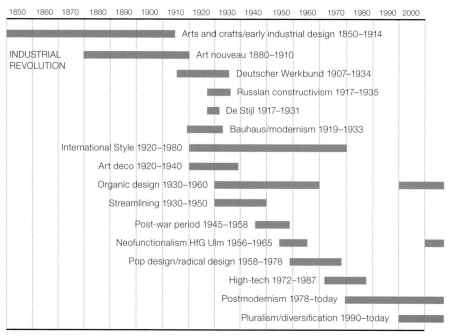

1850 1860 1870 1880 1890 1900 1910 1920 1930 1940 1950 1960 1970 1980 1990 2000

Arts and crafts/early industrial design 1850–1914

INDUSTRIAL REVOLUTION

Art nouveau 1880–1910

Deutscher Werkbund 1907–1934

Russian constructivism 1917–1935

De Stijl 1917–1931

Bauhaus/modernism 1919–1933

International Style 1920–1980

Art deco 1920–1940

Organic design 1930–1960

Streamlining 1930–1950

Post-war period 1945–1958

Neofunctionalism HfG Ulm 1956–1965

Pop design/radical design 1958–1978

High-tech 1972–1987

Postmodernism 1978–today

Pluralism/diversification 1990–today

A mass-produced chair conquers the world

Michael Thonet and the way to industrial mass production
Early industrial design, 1850–1894

Michael Thonet (1796–1871) tried early on to bring wood into a new shape by applying force (bending). He finally succeeded in permanently deforming beech wood rods using pressure and steam. He cleverly exploited the potential of emerging industrialization and developed new production processes that were particularly suitable for industrial mass production. The squared lumber was transported from the sawmill via the turnery to the steam ovens and manually pressed into the iron bending mould. In the drying kilns they then took on their new shape permanently. The basic shapes were standardized and allowed for a wide range of products, from seating furniture, tables and rocking chairs to tennis rackets. The classic among bentwood furniture, however, is the Thonet Chair No. 14, developed in 1859, which is still in production today and has been sold more than 50 million times. It became the epitome of a mass consumer article, which started from the Austro-Hungarian Empire in Vienna and branches in Europe and America. New marketing activities such as printed catalogues, posters and exhibitions at trade fairs promoted sales. In the legendary packaging of the Thonet box (1x1x1 meter), the individual parts of 36 chairs could be protected and stored ready for transport.[4]

Thonet bentwood furniture marked the beginning of a new era in design. The famous architect Le Corbusier said: "Never before has something more elegant and better been created in conception, more precise in execution and more efficient in use."[5]

Thonet Chair No. 14 from 1859

Thonet box with the individual parts of 36 chairs

The first corporate designer forms a corporate image

Peter Behrens, founding member of the Deutscher Werkbund (German Association of Craftsmen), Deutscher Werkbund, 1907–1934

Peter Behrens (1868–1940) was appointed to the artistic advisory board of AEG (Allgemeine Elektricitäts-Gesellschaft) in 1907, where he succeeded in giving the group a uniform appearance over the following years. AEG was one of the world's leading electrical companies, producing turbines and electric motors for industry as well as small household appliances. Today, Behrens is regarded as the first corporate designer because he not only designed the products, but also the lettering, advertising and price lists, all the way to the buildings and sales rooms, in a uniform manner. The turbine hall of the AEG in Berlin can be described as a milestone of modern industrial architecture. When designing table fans, clocks and water boilers, Behrens endeavored to avoid historical styles and ornaments. However, he allowed a reduced use of ornamentation in household products made of valuable materials. The serially produced electric water boiler was available in various shapes, sizes, materials and surfaces. He introduced a typing system with the help of which a wide range of products could be offered.

The Deutscher Werkbund, whose co-founder was Behrens, pursued the goal of establishing new esthetic criteria and thus increasing the quality of German products. It was a union of leading architects, artists and industrialists of the time. The background was the strengthening of the competitiveness of German products on the world market.

Peter Behrens, AEG table fan NGVU 2, around 1910/1912 (middle) and AEG table fan model NOVU 2, around 1930 (left and right)

Loos as a vehement critic: "Ornament and Crime"

Vienna around 1900: a city of arts and art nouveau

Adolf Loos — Wiener Werkstätten — pro or contra ornament

At the turn of the century (around 1900) Vienna was to be established as the capital of good taste. At the same time, artists like Egon Schiele and Gustav Klimt had revolutionized the art world. The architect Josef Hoffmann (1870–1956) founded the Wiener Werkstätten, which produced furniture for a wealthy clientele of emerging industrialists and for the upper middle classes. With the help of high-quality products such as furniture, cutlery, glasses and porcelain, the Wiener Werkstätten wanted to achieve a stylistic influence. However, Adolf Loos (1870–1933) was in critical dialogue with the Wiener Werkstätten. Influenced by his stay in America, the architect built the first unadorned house in the center of Vienna at Michaelaplatz, without ornamental decorations. This building was played up as a scandal and Loos polemicized against this criticism in his own writings. His most important theoretical work "Ornament and Crime" is regarded as a pioneer of modernism and influenced personalities such as Walter Gropius at the later Bauhaus in Weimar. Loos's criticism was directed against historicism and floral art nouveau. His most important insight was that the design of objects of daily use is a separate discipline in its own right and can therefore be clearly separated from art. Many of his contemporaries, such as the aforementioned Josef Hoffmann, saw themselves more as artists and less as product designers or designers, especially since the word design was not yet anchored in the German language.[6]

Adolf Loos, drink service No. 248 produced by Lobmeyr for the American Bar in Vienna, 1931

The cup service has a satin-matt polished brilliant cut on the bottom

The Bauhaus in Dessau, the world's first design school

Bauhaus in Weimar, Dessau and Berlin
Functionalism and modernism, 1918–1932

One of the reasons for the Bauhaus myth is that in a short period of only 14 years (1919–33) it succeeded in establishing itself as the most important school of architecture, design and art in the 20th century. Walter Gropius (1883–1969) was the first director to lay the foundation stone for the idea of functionalism and established the Bauhaus as the center of modernism in Germany. In Dessau, Gropius created a revolutionary new building that was occupied in 1925 and whose spatial concept was based on uniting all areas of life such as working, living, learning, sport and entertainment under one roof. The unadorned building complex in Dessau is dominated by transparency, especially the self-supporting glass facade of the workshop wing, which extends over three stories. Gropius envisions a new unity of art, craftsmanship and industry: "The Bauhaus strives to unite all artistic creation into one unity, the reunification of all practical art disciplines – sculpture, painting, arts and crafts and handicrafts – into a new architectural art as its indissoluble components."[7]

In the Bauhaus philosophy, architecture and design have above all a social purpose, in that elementary needs such as housing and corresponding furniture should be available to many people at low cost. Under the motto "Art and technology – a new unit", furniture and utensils were designed for serial production. With the help of typing and standardization, products were developed that were suitable for mass production.

Walter Gropius, Bauhaus building, workshop wing (self-supporting glass facade), Dessau 1925/26

Under the second director of the Bauhaus, the Swiss architect Hannes Mayer, the Bauhaus underwent a transformation into a "university of design". No value-free artistic individual works were propagated, but rather everyday objects that were to be produced in cooperation with industry. Mayer was primarily concerned with the question of how well-designed products and buildings could be realized in order to be affordable for everyone. Under Mayer, many students radicalized themselves and committed themselves to communism. Mayer had to leave the Bauhaus in 1930 under political pressure and emigrated to Moscow with 12 students.

Ludwig Mies van der Rohe (1886–1969) was appointed third director of the Bauhaus in 1930, but had to close it in 1932 under pressure from the National Socialists. He then tried to continue the Bauhaus as a private institute in Berlin, but after many conflicts with the National Socialists in 1933 Mies van der Rohe had to announce the dissolution of the Bauhaus. After he had emigrated to America in 1938, he took over the architectural department of the later Illinois Institute of Technology.

The expression "less is more" by Ludwig Mies van der Rohe stands for functionalism and shows that the economy of means guarantees cost-effective production and that the "purity" of form is also associated with "beauty".

Marcel Breuer was one of the most important protagonists at the Bauhaus and designed his first tubular steel furniture, which became icons of modernism. His most famous design is the "Wassily Chair", created in 1925/26.

The politically motivated emigration of students and teachers could not destroy the idea of the Bauhaus, but rather led to a worldwide further development of research, teaching and design practice. The students, who came to the Bauhaus from 29 countries, spread the idea in their countries of origin.

Marcel Breuer, club chair Wassily Chair, second version, 1926

The first star designer makes styling popular in America

Raymond Loewy and the streamline
Streamline shape, 1933–1945

Streamline is inextricably linked with America's most famous designer, Raymond Loewy (1893–1986). Born in Paris, Loewy went to New York at the end of the First World War, where he first worked as a fashion designer and opened his own office for industrial design in 1929. With his penchant for self-portrayal and egocentricity, he quickly rose to become an American star designer. In times of the global economic crisis and the associated decline in sales figures, he has skillfully understood how to suggest needs and arouse consumers' buying interest. His design principle was not derived from the function of a product, but from the streamlined form, which has meanwhile been frowned upon as styling, suggesting dynamism, belief in progress and optimism. Loewy acted as a consultant designer who used styling to boost sales of obsolete products. His famous pencil sharpener in the shape of an aircraft engine shows that a purely stationary product suddenly experiences a dynamic force and the shiny surface radiates a lot of glamour.

Loewy was a public relation talent who contributed a lot to awakening design awareness in the American public. In his 1951 book "Never leave well enough alone" he wrote: "My products should have a certain monumentality and a certain amount of glamour."

Raymond Loewy in front of a wall with the trademarks of his numerous customers

Pencil sharpener by Raymond Loewy in the shape of an aircraft engine, 1933

Organic design with soft and flowing shapes

Charles Eames and Eero Saarinen experiment with plywood
Organic design, 1930–1960

The MoMA (Museum of Modern Art) in New York had already built up a design collection in the 1930s and became an American design institution through exhibitions and competitions. "Organic Design in Home Furnishing" was the name of the 1940 design competition won by Charles Eames (1907–1978) and Eero Saarinen (1910–1961), who had already gained experience in designing furniture with organic shapes. The following organic design exhibition (1941) was a collection of prototypes and small series for which there were no mass production processes. Only through the collaboration of Charles Eames with his wife Ray was it possible to develop a new production method for organically shaped plywood chairs. In the so-called Kazam! Machine, a mould made of plaster, heating wires were inserted, which made it possible to shape plywood into the desired shape in several layers of veneer and glue. With this material innovation they received an order from the US Navy for the production of leg splints and stretchers for use with wounded soldiers. Ray and Charles Eames cultivated a playful approach to materials such as fiberglass, plastic and plywood and created design icons from them, which are still very successfully produced by Hermann Miller in the USA and by Vitra in Germany. Their work was based on passion, creativity, but also seriousness, which is very well expressed in her maxim "take your pleasure seriously."

Charles and Ray Eames: Lounge Chair & Ottoman, 1956; Occasional Table (Low Table Rod Base), 1950; Eames Plastic Armchair (Rocking Armchair Rod Base), 1950; Eames Elephant (Plywood), 1945

"From the cooking spoon to the city"

Good design
The Hochschule für Gestaltung in Ulm (HfG), 1953–1969

After the end of the Second World War, a foundation was established in memory of the siblings Hans and Sophie Scholl (White Rose resistance group) murdered by the National Socialists. This Geschwister Scholl Foundation developed into the HfG Ulm, which followed the tradition of the Bauhaus. The aim was to establish a new culture of functional beauty "from the cooking spoon to the city" (quote by Max Bill). Due to their democratic self-image, students were granted the right to co-determination as early as 1955. There were four divisions: product design, information, visual communication and industrial construction. The HfG Ulm successively scientified the design, developed a methodology for product planning, accelerated the integration of ergonomics (work physiology) into the design process and developed a system design oriented towards mass production. Unlike at the Bauhaus, the curriculum was not tied to a master class principle, but was rather oriented towards the natural and engineering sciences with exact findings. There was no actual artistic training. The curriculum included disciplines such as ergonomics, mathematics, economics, physics and semiotics. This strong rationalism and the scientification of design, which turned against artistic aspects of design, led to tensions. Max Bill eventually resigned as rector and, in addition, by cancelling state funding a lack of money aggravated the crisis. The high ethical standards of the school in environmental design and conflicts between the Geschwister Scholl Foundation and politics led to the closure of the HfG Ulm in 1968.

form follows function

Louis Sullivan, 1896

less is more

Ludwig Mies van der Rohe, 1947

less but better

Dieter Rams, 1970s

Dieter Rams and his principle: "Less but better"

Braun design
Neofunctionalism, 1956–1965

From the 1960s onwards, representatives of HfG Ulm developed communication systems and corporate identities for companies in the form of a concise corporate identity. Otl Aicher designed the appearance of the Lufthansa brand, which is still in use today with only minor adaptations. Furthermore, for the 1972 Olympic Games in Munich he created reduced pictograms, a universal sign language, i.e., for the first time a comprehensive appearance for a sports event. His design theoretical publications are important foundations for the field of visual communication. In terms of product design, the Braun company consistently implemented the "Ulm style", which was based on the esthetics of constructivism and functionalism. Clear geometric shapes, combined with the idea of unobtrusive restraint, gave the products a timeless charm. Dieter Rams was appointed director of the design department in 1961 and is regarded as one of the most important industrial designers in Germany. He shaped the image of Braun AG by combining the technologically advanced products into product families and systems and building up a strong image by means of a uniform communication system. The motto of Dieter Rams is "Less design is more design"[8], with which he has taken up and expanded the thoughts of Mies van der Rohe and his motto "Less is more". Dieter Rams has been a professor of industrial design in Hamburg since 1981 and received an honorary doctorate from the London Royal Collage of Art in 1991. In 1999 he became a member of the Akademie der Künste (Academy of Arts) in Berlin.

Dieter Rams, Braun design

Phono transistor TP1 by Dieter Rams, 1959

A colorful world at the time of the moon landing

Verner Panton and his room installations
Pop culture of the 1960s and 1970s

Student unrest in Europe, the hippie culture in America – these were the 1960s, a time of social and political upheavals. At the same time the moon landing (1968) spread an enormous atmosphere of departure and a noticeable euphoria. In the western industrial nations there was strong criticism of the capitalist economic system, the associated environmental pollution and unequal distribution of wealth. Perhaps it was precisely as a reaction to this attitude of protest that a new organic, colorful design world prevailed. Verner Panton (1926–1998) had the idea of a sensual living landscape far removed from all traditional habits and created his spatial installation Visiona 2, which was shown at the Cologne Furniture Fair. Verner Panton radically dissolved the separate functions of living, sleeping, eating etc. and merged the rooms seamlessly into one another. He also dissolved the spatial structure of floor, wall and ceiling, creating an expansive living landscape with colorful lights, scents, video projections and music. The spatial experience was much more open and democratic, but also more emotional, because all sensory organs were addressed. The organic forms found their expression in soft materials and convey a sense of security and relaxation.

Panton's persistent handling of material was the reason for the first cantilever chair, which was made of one material, one casting, and plastic throughout. The Panton Chair (1959/60–1968) is the design icon of its time, the implementation of which could only be realized through the development of new plastics over several years.

Verner Panton
Futuristic living landscape (Phantasy Landscape), Visiona 2, at the Cologne Furniture Fair, 1970

Questioning modernity by postmodernism

Ettore Sottsass and Memphis Design
Postmodernism, 1976 to date

The French philosopher Jean-François Lyotard coined the term postmodernism in 1979, which subsequently found its way into architecture and design. Postmodernism demanded a radical plurality that, in addition to rationality, has also allowed emotionality, deconstruction, construction, and future orientation, as well as recourse to the past. Towards the end of the 1960s, the conventions of "good form" or "kitsch" and "high culture" or "everyday culture" were dissolved. This was the beginning of diversification in design. The driving force behind this movement were designers from Italy who turned against "Bel Design". Ettore Sottsass (1917–2007) became an outstanding personality, who was co-founder of the Memphis group along with Matteo Thun, Michele de Lucchi and others. The Memphis objects had nothing to do with usefulness and practical functions. They were stylized into design objects that moved between pop art and kitsch. They contrast the uniformity of functionalism with colorfulness and symbolic design. Style quotations from past epochs as well as lavish ornaments shaped the products. The very rational esthetics of modernism were extended by a conscious signification of the objects in postmodernism. An excellent theoretical reflection on semiotics (sign theory) was provided by the Italian writer Umberto Eco with his work "Einführung in die Semiotik" (1988).

Ettore Sottsass designed the Olivetti Valentine typewriter by Memphis Design, 1969

Ettore Sottsass in 1998 behind his room divider Carlton by Memphis Design, 1981

Mutual inspiration of nature, science and technology

Research and design/CAD Computer Aided Design
High-tech design, 1970s and 1980s

In the history of design, design and technological innovations are inextricably linked. Since the mid-1970s, technological developments have given rise to a new esthetic that has established itself under the term "high-tech" and was named after the publication of the same name by Suzanne Slesin and Joan Kron (1979). The Centre Pompidou (1971–1977) in Paris by Richard Rogers and Renzo Piano, also plays with this high-tech esthetic and sets a modern counterpoint in the historical cityscape. The office furniture system Nomos (1986) by Lord Norman Foster also shows a mixture of high precision and the use of new constructions and materials. Nomos is manufactured by the Italian furniture manufacturer Teco spa. Foster + Partners is the architecture and design studio founded by Lord Norman Foster in 1967 in London, with worldwide projects such as the 2017 opened Steve Jobs Theatre in Cupertino.

Since the 1990s, the shift in product design and engineering from the analog drawing table to digital tools has resulted in a new language of form that is closely linked to these new digital tools. Organic or biomorphic forms such as mussels, nets or cell structures are created with the help of computers and corresponding software and thus expand the spectrum of possible forms. Structures in nature are often a model for the construction of machines or products.

High-tech workstation with the Nomos office furniture system by Lord Norman Foster, 1986

High-tech architecture by Richard Rogers and Renzo Piano, Centre Pompidou in Paris, 1971–1977

Surfing the Internet with iMac in "Bondi Blue" color

Steve Jobs and Apple design
Jonathan Ive — Apple design

For the late 20th century, digitization and advances in microelectronics are the key drivers of design. In the world of office workplaces, the computer with e-mail and the Internet is becoming more and more popular. The PCs of that time are not coordinated systems, but are often configured individually; computer, monitor, operating system and user software are supplied by different manufacturers. Correspondingly error-prone during installation and slow in operation, these computers often cause frustration among users. Apple is entering this gap and is developing the first iMac generation, in which screen, PC and the user-friendly operating system merge into a single unit (all-in-one computer). In 1992, London-born designer Jonathan Ive joined Apple and set up a design department. After the return of Steve Jobs in 1997, the iMac was launched the following year, which made "surfing the Internet" simple and fast for the first time. It differed considerably from the beige-colored computers common at that time, thanks to its translucent plastic case in various colors. The emotional design with the soft form and the color "Bondi Blue" as well as the unusual naming caused a sensation.

Apple iMac by Jonathan Ive, 1998

List of sources:

(1) Sullivan, Louis H.: The Tall Office Building Artistically Considered, in: Lippicott's, March 1896
(2) Bürdek, Bernhard E.: Design: Geschichte, Theorie und Praxis der Produktgestaltung, Birkhäuser Verlag, Cologne, 2015
(3) Bürdek, Bernhard E.: Design: Geschichte, Theorie und Praxis der Produktgestaltung, Birkhäuser Verlag, Cologne, 1991
(4) Berents, Catharina: Kleine Geschichte des Design, Verlag C.H.Beck, Munich, 2011
(5) Hauffe, Thomas: Geschichte des Designs, DuMont Buchverlag, Cologne, 2014
(6) Loos, Adolf: Ornament & Vebrechen (Ed. Peter Stuiber), Metroverlag, Vienna, 2012
(7) Gropius, Walter – from the program of the "Manifesto of the Staatliches Bauhaus", Weimar, 1919
(8) Rams, Dieter: Weniger aber besser, Jo Klatt Design+Design Verlag, Hamburg, 1995

Design disciplines

There is no universal, scientifically justifiable subdivision of design into strict disciplines. At colleges and academies, the arts and crafts traditions with their focus on materials still frequently formed the basis for any structuring up to the first half of the 20th century. Consequently, they offered master classes in wood, metal, ceramics, glass, textiles, etc. Given the changes seen in the profession over the years, five major fields have now emerged:

- **Product design**
- **Transportation design**
- **Fashion design**
- **Exhibition design/interior design**
- **Communication design**

Industrial design as a collective term encompasses all design disciplines that are closely related to industrial manufacturing processes. Industrial designers work in special fields that are assigned to product design, transportation design or others. They deal with the manufacture of certain products, from motorcycles to sporting goods and household appliances. Specialization can also be applied to complex products with a high proportion of electronics, such as medical technology, mobile phones or laptops. When packaging design focuses on product-oriented design such as 3-D folding boxes or packaging for cleaning agents with a spray function, this is also referred to as product design. In practice, the terms industrial design and product design are often used equivalently, although industrial design is regarded as the superordinate term.

KISKA VISION FUTURE SAILING, master thesis by Simon Bildstein, FH JOANNEUM Industrial Design in cooperation with KISKA (Transportation Design).
An innovative catamaran concept whose deck platform offers a luxurious living space like on a sailing yacht. At the same time, the exclusive "Daysailer" has the dynamics of a racing catamaran.
Supervisor: Marc Ischepp, FH JOANNEUM and Christopher Gloning, KISKA

PEEL, for peeling fruit and vegetables (consumer goods). Project work "Cooking/innovative kitchen appliances" in cooperation with Philips. Design: Constantin Mödl
Supervisor: Johannes Scherr, FH JOANNEUM

CETUS, a fully automatic wood shredder (capital goods). Project work "Schredder der Zukunft" (Shredder of the Future) in cooperation with KOMPTECH. Design: Christoph Andrejcic and Maximilian Troicher
Supervisors: Johannes Scherr and Gerald Steiner, FH JOANNEUM Industrial Design

In **product design**, we differentiate between the design of consumer goods and capital goods. Consumer goods are mainly found in households and are produced for private consumption in the areas of sport, leisure, entertainment, etc. Capital goods are usually intended for the production process and include production machines such as saws, milling machines, printing machines, etc. or medical and measurement equipment.

Transportation design deals with automotive design, motorcycle design, aircraft design, yacht design, etc., basically everything that moves on land, in the water and in the air. Due to the complexity of the products, transportation design has various specializations such as exterior and interior design. There are also areas for color and trim, light design, engine compartment design, interface design and many more.

BENELLI MIA, a big city quad for the individual traffic of the future (transportation design).
Design: Hannah Katzlberger, Marc Korbuly, Stefan Märzendorfer, FH JOANNEUM Industrial Design
Supervisors: Lutz Kucher and Julian Herget (Design), Georg Wagner (Engineering) FH JOANNEUM

Exhibition design deals with trade fair presentations, design, art and world exhibitions, scenographic design of museums and collections, etc.

The Milan Furniture Fair in Italy is an important meeting place for the international design scene. It is considered the most important furniture fair in the world, with numerous automobile manufacturers and important brand labels also presenting their new developments and trends there.

Interior design is dedicated to interior architecture, shop design (planning and design of business premises such as shops or restaurants), etc.

Interior design is not only about equipping surfaces such as walls, floors and ceilings, but especially about questions of user behavior, technical equipment (climate, lighting, multimedia, etc.), ecological construction, coordination with architecture and the environment.

Furniture design has a long historical tradition and includes many classics by designers and architects. Today, office chairs with ergonomic requirements are designed by product, interior, industrial designers or architects.

Fashion design includes clothing, shoes, accessories as well as jewelry and textile design. On the one hand, it describes the haute couture centers in the USA, Europe and Japan. On the other hand, street styles of various subcultures such as hippies, punks and skins developed into New Romantics. Historically, designer Mary Quant invented the mini skirt in the 1960s, triggering a social revolution.

Communication design deals with information design, media design, graphic design, web design (conception, design and structure of websites with corresponding navigation and user guidance), etc.

Industrial Design Show is the annual exhibition of the FH JOANNEUM Industrial Design at designforum steiermark (left) and Kunsthaus Graz (right).

The print medium Design Mail of FH JOANNEUM Industrial Design contains documentation of current project, bachelor and master theses. An example of communication design, www.fh-joanneum.at

In industrial design, a number of terms have established themselves that are indispensable, among other things, in the design of electronic devices. Some terms are defined here in order to create a better understanding.

The focus of every design process is always the user, i.e., the person who operates a product, navigates on a touch screen or drives a vehicle. Designers therefore ask themselves how good the **usability** of products and systems is. The term usability originally comes from ergonomics and was used to analyze the human-machine interface. Today, usability has an extended spectrum of meaning and describes all interactions between people (users) and their designed environment. It includes products, user interfaces (screen/touch screen), but also services and experiences. Designers are confronted with the challenge of taking these complex needs and expectations of users into account in the design process as well as people's behavior when operating and using products.

In recent years, the term **user-centered design** has developed from this topic area. The aim is to improve the usability of products and services in applications by analyzing and constantly improving the experience of end users in the design process. It is therefore essential to involve future users in the design right from the start. For example, the logical and intuitive handling procedure is examined. When designing a product, a website, an app, etc., the designer can therefore focus on the needs, expectations, wishes and understanding of the future user.

In addition to the term user-centered design, we often find a shift towards **human-centered design** in practice. This conscious change in design philosophy places the human factor even more at the center of the design process. It is about focusing on the human being as a whole with all his sensual perceptions.

User-centered design is becoming increasingly important for complex systems such as autonomous (self-propelled) vehicles. With this design, the passenger can retreat, enjoy the view or intensively experience the dynamics and speed of driving in the front row. Many services can be accessed via the interface of a central office.

Master thesis by Isabella Zidek in cooperation with BMW Group Interieur Design. Design: Isabella Zidek, supervisor: Michael Lanz, FH JOANNEUM Industrial Design and Christian Bauer, BMW Munich.

In product design, we are experiencing an ever-stronger fusion of hardware and software elements. Let's think of a smartphone that usually consists of a very functional, monochrome case and innumerable messenger services, apps and additional functions inside. Here we can see the importance of **interface design** in product design. An emphasis of interface design lies, as the name suggests, in the design of the interfaces from analog to digital content. It is about the concrete visible design on the monitor, display or touch screen, but also about switching or operating elements, i.e., the user interfaces of hardware or software. In addition, product designers strive to merge these analog and digital interfaces of a product into a sensual overall experience. Complex systems such as mobile phones, navigation systems, computers or websites are only accepted by the user if the interface design responds to his needs and behavior. Therefore, the integration of interface design into the design process is the key to success.

Two fields of work that have developed from interface design are experience design and interaction design. The former is referred to in the application as **user experience (UX)** and describes the perceptions and reactions of people when using a product. This refers to the emotions of the users, the psychological and physiological reactions, the expectations in dealing with the product. The term describes everything we come into contact with when using the product. This does not only mean the operation of a product, but also how it is packaged and how it is ultimately recycled after use.

The challenge in designing an interface may be that an eight-year-old child can handle it as well as an 80-year-old person. This applies, for example, to products such as a smart home system for controlling technical equipment in the house, including heating, shading, entertainment, etc. as well as the associated monitoring systems. Here the interface designer

User interface (UI), user experience (UX) in the application of an infant monitoring system. This home monitoring system designed specifically for newborns provides parents with the confidence they need to monitor their high-risk infant on a daily basis. UI/UX is an essential component of the home monitoring system. The product was redesigned starting with the packaging, through the introduction to the handling of the device, to the evaluation of the data. A detailed description of the master thesis and the design process can be found on pages 160 to 169.
Master thesis by Christina Wolf at FH JOANNEUM Industrial Design in cooperation with Getemed.
Supervisor: Johannes Scherr, FH JOANNEUM Industrial Design

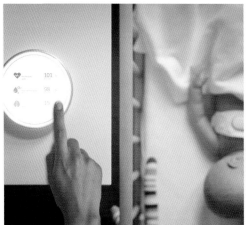
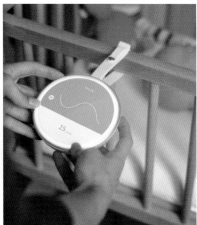

is often faced with the question of how many keys are required on the hardware to achieve the optimal user experience or which restrictive elements and standards have to be taken into account. Many questions that only lead to an innovative product in the interaction of product design and interaction design.

Interaction design[1] is an integral part of interface design and describes the dialogue between the user and the digital applications as a system that can respond with feedback to the user's input, articulation or selection. Interaction design deals with the design of these processes, i.e., the temporal dimension of interaction. The art lies in combining deeply anchored analog actions with new digital content.

In addition to the design disciplines described so far, other areas have developed in the recent past, above all as a result of social changes. The change from an industrial society to an information and service-oriented society has resulted in new areas of responsibility for design. The share of services in Austria's gross domestic product (GDP) is already 70 percent. Therefore, the number of start-ups in this sector is rising sharply.

The term **service design** makes it clear that services also require design. By service design we mean the process of designing services. The main focus is on the functionality and form of services from the customer's perspective. The needs and behaviors of customers are monitored in order to derive innovative and marketable services or to improve existing services. The material and immaterial touch points of the customer with the service offer, the entire user guidance, as well as the underlying organizational process are designed above all.

An example of **service design** is the concept of the Philips Bar, which is not only a product, but also offers an extensive range of services. Philips provides the hardware for the product and the entire cooking and eating experience. The user decides what to eat and learns in a playful way how to prepare the food quickly and easily, creating new services that can be accessed via apps or websites.
Project work "Cooking with Air", FH JOANNEUM in cooperation with Philips Austria GmbH.
Design: Robert Klos, third semester bachelor studies FH JOANNEUM Industrial Design
Supervisors: Johannes Scherr (Design) and Matthias Götz (Ergonomics), FH JOANNEUM Industrial Design

menu   dishes   product

Since the emergence of a growing awareness of environmental problems in the 1970s, designers have also been dealing with environmental and social issues, e.g., under the title **eco design** or **design for sustainability**. Sustainable development, as defined by the so-called Brundtland Commission of the United Nations, aims to enable the long-term survival of a growing world population on our planet with limited resources and to create the necessary ecological, economic and social conditions. The alarming reports on climate change, scarcity of resources and social injustice not only concern politicians and entrepreneurs, but also an ever wider range of the population. In response to these global developments, the **"eco-innovative design"** specialization[2] was established in the Industrial Design master program at FH JOANNEUM to sensitize students to these topics.

Eco-innovative design integrates the fields of ecology and innovation into the design of products, systems, services and experiences. The aim is to counteract the progressive destruction of our environment and to generate solutions that are good for people and the natural environment. At the same time, the aim is to create added value for as many people as possible. Aspects such as minimized resource consumption, use of regenerative energy, recycling management and socially acceptable production conditions are taken into account right from the start of product development in the design process. The end result are innovative and attractive solutions that encourage users to use them in an ecologically and socially meaningful way and help the respective target groups to make their lifestyles more sustainable.

The FUSION project is an example from the **eco-innovative design** research. The task was the development of flexible partitioning systems for the one-room house of Baufritz. The basic body serves as storage space and can also be used as seating furniture. The different color and material options make the design an individual experience, whereby only ecologically sustainable materials such as wood, felt, etc. are available.

Project work "Flexible Raumtrenn- und Möbelsysteme" (Flexible Room Partitioning and Furniture Systems) at FH JOANNEUM Industrial Design in cooperation with Baufritz – Ökohaus Pionier.
Design: Christoph Andrejcic and Simon Schuster, FH JOANNEUM Industrial Design
Supervisor: Ursula Tischner and Michael Lanz, FH JOANNEUM Industrial Design

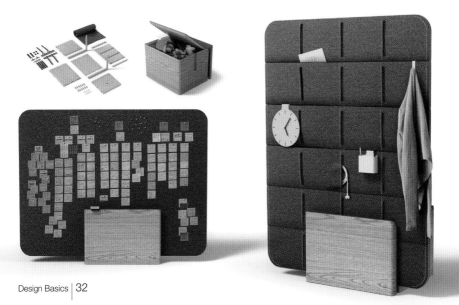

Mobility is a human need – both socially and individually. In many areas, however, we are reaching the limits of the performance of our transport systems due to a greater need for mobility and population growth. For this reason, the second specialization **"mobility design"** was established in the Industrial Design master program at FH JOANNEUM. This project investigates how an intelligent design of means of transport and transport systems can combine ecological goals, industrial process requirements and regionally different mobility needs to form new, meaningful overall concepts.

We present the RECUBE project as an example of the **mobility design** specialization. The task here was to design an urban mobility concept. The idea was to develop a service for the supermarket in which the goods are delivered quickly and cheaply, without any negative impact on the environment. Payment is made by charging the battery return boxes, which the customer exchanges with the supplier upon delivery. The refrigerated transport boxes are mainly delivered to the city center by the electrically operated delivery van.

Project work entitled "Fahrzeugkonzepte für urbane Mobilität" (Vehicle Concepts for Urban Mobility) in cooperation with Schaeffler.
Design: Lennart Baramsky, Frieder Heitmann, Maximilian Resch, FH JOANNEUM Industrial Design
Supervisors: Michael Lanz, Bernd Stelzer, Miltos Oliver Kountouras, FH JOANNEUM Industrial Design

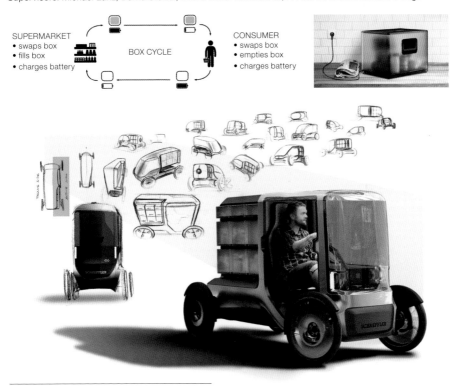

SUPERMARKET
• swaps box
• fills box
• charges battery

BOX CYCLE

CONSUMER
• swaps box
• empties box
• charges battery

List of sources:

(1) Erlhoff, Michael/Marshall, Tim: Wörterbuch Design. Birkhäuser Verlag, Basel/Boston/Berlin, 2008
(2) Tischner, Ursula et al.: Was ist EcoDesign? Birkhäuser Verlag, Basel, 2000

Definition of design

At the 29th General Assembly of the World Design Organisation (WDO) in Gwangju (South Korea), the following renewed definition of industrial design was unveiled:

> **Industrial design is a strategic problem-solving process that drives innovation, builds business success, and leads to a better quality of life through innovative products, systems, services, and experiences.**

In a more detailed version the following aspects are added:

Industrial design is a strategic problem-solving process that drives innovation, builds business success, and leads to a better quality of life through innovative products, systems, services, and experiences. Industrial Design bridges the gap between what is and what's possible. It is a trans-disciplinary profession that harnesses creativity to resolve problems and co-create solutions with the intent of making a product, system, service, experience or a business, better. At its heart, Industrial Design provides a more optimistic way of looking at the future by reframing problems as opportunities. It links innovation, technology, research, business, and customers to provide new value and competitive advantage across economic, social, and environmental spheres.

Industrial designers place the human in the center of the process. They acquire a deep understanding of user needs through empathy and apply a pragmatic, user-centric problem-solving process to design products, systems, services, and experiences. They are strategic stakeholders in the innovation process and are uniquely positioned to bridge varied professional disciplines and business interests. They value the economic, social, and environmental impact of their work and their contribution towards co-creating a better quality of life.[1]

Therefore, the term "designer" refers to an individual who practices an intellectual profession, and not simply a trade or a service for enterprises.

List of sources:

(1) http://wdo.org/about/definition

In order to allow a further definition of the term "industrial design", we can summarize:

Industrial design is the planning of industrially manufacturable products or systems. A holistic problem-solving process, industrial design aims on the one hand to adapt consumer goods to the users' needs, and on the other to meet the demands of the market, corporate identity and economic manufacture for the entrepreneurs. Furthermore, industrial design is a cultural, social and ecological factor.

According to WDO's most recent definition, industrial design includes not only products but also systems, services and user experiences. The developments of the last 25 years with innovations in the fields of smart materials, 3-D printing processes, microprocessors, artificial intelligence and, of course, the Internet have expanded the term industrial design in many ways. In the age of industry 4.0, the term "industrial", in reference to the industrial revolution, already seems outdated. Nevertheless, the term "industrial design" has established itself in the university sector for corresponding courses of study (alongside other terms such as "product design").

Another word which frequently crops up in this context is **styling**. The term is still often confused with design in the media, and in some companies the design department is called the styling department. So what is the difference?
Let us first take a look at the historic roots of styling: USA – at the end of the 1920s – the Wall Street Crash – the Great Depression. The consumers' lack of spending left companies sitting on their products. When the economic situation slowly started to recover in the course of the 1930s, many companies were faced with a problem: they still had large stocks of products that were fully functional technically, but outdated in appearance. They therefore quickly gave the products a new exterior or makeover while leaving the core untouched. This was the birth of styling, which has since been used as a short-term fashion wave not only in the United States, but also worldwide and is often called a "look" (e.g., "futuristic look", "ethnic look", etc.).

Styling is cosmetic treatment limited to the surface of the product.

The focus is on aspects of form rather than practical functions and it therefore tends to have a one-sided show character. In colloquial use, styling is often mistakenly equated with design.

In today's age of saturated markets, anyone who wants to boost the sale of a product can use redesign. Through esthetic differentiation, a competitive advantage is achieved by building on the familiarity of the introduced product language. Similarly, a technical innovation that has established itself on the market may require a redesign. If new manufacturing methods are introduced in the manufacturing process of a product, a redesign should also be aimed at. So when it comes to revising products that are already on the market, the term redesign is appropriate.

Redesign is the creative revision of an existing product, whereby the collected experiences from product development, production and market feedback flow into the following model. It uses the awareness of the existing product and increases the competitiveness of the successor. Redesign is a way to react to changing needs and technical innovations.

The pictures show the redesign of a hairdryer and a Braun juicer. A new switch button has been developed for the hairdryer and the product graphics have been changed. With the juicer, the functionality of operation and the possibility of cleaning were improved. The basic shape remained the same, the large radii on the edges are conspicuous. At the front there is an indentation for the glass into which the juice flows. A horizontal joint separates the press from the motor housing. It is a switchless device in which the motor is activated by the pressure triggered during pressing.

Braun hairdryer HLD 231
Design: Reinhold Weiss, 1964

Braun hairdryer HLD 3
Design: Reinhold Weiss, 1972

Braun juicer Multipress MP 32
Design: Gerd A. Müller, 1965

Braun juicer Multipress MP 50
Design: Jürgen Greubel, 1970

Industrial design as a profession

Industrial designers can offer their services as employees in a company's own development department, as members of a design office staff, or as freelancers. The scope of their activities lies in planning the creation of industrially manufactured products and product systems in close cooperation with interdisciplinary development teams.

There are many designers worldwide who primarily concentrate on esthetically-oriented object design. On the other hand, there is a lack of designers who understand the language of constructors or electronic engineers as well as that of marketing or ergonomics experts.

Industry therefore expects of a designer:
- **Creativity in the sense of problem-solving skills**
- **Ability to draw concepts and plans**
- **Skills in computer-aided 3-D design** (the common tools Alias, Rhino, Solid Works)
- **Knowledge of semantics** (product language in relation to design)
- **Skills in ergonomics, usability and interface design**
- **Working knowledge of engineering from mechanical to electronic**
- **Basic knowledge of manufacturing processes**
- **Economic thinking**
- **Sustainable thinking** (ecology, economy, sociology)
- **Capacity for teamwork and dedication**
- **Independent, responsible thinking and acting**

In addition, society expects designers also to assume the cultural responsibility inherent in the cycle of creation:

We form our environment, and the environment forms us!

When developing products, it is essential to work together with different disciplines. The ability to work in a team and commitment are important character traits in order to ultimately design a high-quality product. In all projects of the Industrial Design course, special attention is paid to these skills.

Project work "MAN High Efficiency Coach": group picture with the cooperation partners of MAN Bus & Truck AG and the advisors of FH JOANNEUM (left).
Final presentation at the end of the semester of the real model with institute director Michael Lanz, students and company representatives from MAN Bus & Truck AG (right).

What is the added value of design?

Design and company

Preliminary remarks

A key event at the beginning of the 21st century was certainly the presentation of the first Apple smartphone by Steve Jobs in 2007. From an entrepreneurial perspective, it was astounding that a manufacturer of computers such as Apple was entering a saturated market of mobile phone providers and was able to achieve enormous success. At the time, there were a number of market leaders in mobile handset suppliers such as Nokia, Motorola, Samsung and others in a market that was only seemingly saturated. Who among the industry leaders at that time would have thought that mobile telephony was facing revolutionary changes? Nokia, in particular, has suffered major losses, but is still economically very successful due to the sale of simple phones in emerging markets. The market leadership is now shared by Apple, HTC, Huawai, Samsung, Sony and others, who are in a tough competition.

Looking back, two factors were certainly of enormous importance for this development: **design and innovation.**

Today's smartphone developed from the simple idea of being able to type on a touch screen like on a computer keyboard. In principle, it is a portable computer with a multitude of functions that, in the age of globalization, makes our digital processes possible in a global network.

This example shows that companies can stand out through innovative design, make product improvements clear and thus achieve a competitive advantage. For most globally operating large companies, it is no longer conceivable to survive on the world market without design. Design is an essential component of the company here and is often strategically influentially positioned at the highest management level within the group. This development shows the high value that design has gained over the past decades. The position of chief design officer (CDO), which companies such as Apple, Kia, Philips, etc. have already successfully installed, bundles all aspects of design and reports directly to the executive board. In the 1990s, design departments were still subordinate to the head of marketing or were located at a lower decision-making level in the area of product development.

In addition to creating their own in-house design department, companies also have the opportunity to work with a design studio that operates independently of their own company. In the field of small and medium-sized enterprises (SMEs), design often does not yet have a pronounced significance, and there is development potential here. Precisely because these companies do not offer mass products, but solutions for a very specific market segment, design can significantly support entrepreneurial objectives.

However, product design must never be an isolated measure. Design is an essential component in the process of product development, influences entrepreneurial success or failure and must be supported by the entire team. In other words, no matter how well designed a product may be, if all other measures – from internal presentation to external marketing – are not right, it can still be a flop. This means that design must become an integral part of the corporate philosophy so that one can also speak of a comprehensive corporate culture.

But let's get back to the concrete question:
What added value can design bring to a company? Answers are given below:

Most important message: **DESIGN BRINGS COMPETITIVE ADVANTAGES!**

Design as a strategic tool

Reducing design solely to the design of products is certainly not enough under tough competitive conditions. Design has become the strategic factor of a successful company. Gerald Kiska (owner of the KISKA design studio) answers the question of what exactly is KISKA today – a design agency, brand developer or communications agency:

"Together with our customers, we create distinctive brand experiences. That's a big promise, of course. And this requires a wide range of different services and a great depth of know-how. We make both available to our customers. This becomes clearest with KTM."[1]

What this means is that KISKA offers a wide range of services, from research and consulting to transportation, graphics, interface and product design. In addition to all these specializations and complex requirements in the age of digitization, the igniting IDEA is still needed. Gerald Kiska comments on this on the first page of his book "Designing Desire":

"It starts with an IDEA. And then you need one thing above all else: courage."

List of sources:

(1) Kiska, Gerald (ed.): Designing Desire – 25 Years Kiska, Anif/Salzburg, 2015

In his book "Designing Desire", Gerald Kiska and his multidisciplinary team present design masterpieces from 25 years of design studio KISKA. As the title reveals, it's about wishes, longings and desires that are addressed by design. To awaken these needs, however, a design strategy is needed.

The term "strategy" originally comes from the military environment and describes the art of army command. For the leader of an army, the goal is always clearly defined: to defeat the enemy. In business, the term strategy naturally has a slightly different meaning. It's about promoting a company's performance and efficiency, and it's about designers, customers and the competition, thus everyone involved. Continuous measures such as strategic design should strengthen the innovative ability and competitiveness of a company or organization. What used to be demanded of generals in former times and of entrepreneurs and management today in principle means the same in implementation, which is courage! Courage in the consistent implementation of an idea.

When an idea turns into a product, design is an essential element of this strategy. At the end of the day, these actions generate added value for all involved, namely the entrepreneurs, designers and customers. It is a matter of comparing oneself with the competitors in a positive competition and achieving a competitive advantage in the strategic sense. Design thus becomes a strategic instrument.

The NOMAD concept can be described as an **"unmistakable brand experience"** with an adventurous character. NOMAD creates new riding experiences through digital networking between base station, rider and motorcycle. The base station is a four-wheeled autonomous vehicle with energy sources such as generator, solar tent and battery modules. Starting from the base station, excursions with the electric motorbike to the most difficult terrain are undertaken. The development of driverless cars makes it possible to pick up the motorcyclist at his position.
Project work "KTM Move Extreme" at FH JOANNEUM in cooperation with KTM and KISKA.
Design: Lukas Wagner, FH JOANNEUM Industrial Design
Supervisors: Michael Lanz, Marc Ischepp, Lutz Kucher, FH JOANNEUM and Christof Täubl, KISKA

Design creates innovation

Innovation is derived from the Latin verb *innovare* (renew), whereby innovation in connection with design is not understood as mere "novelty". One example of innovation is the development of the smartphone mentioned above. With the smartphone, the touch screen technology available on the market was to replace the keyboard previously used for entering data on a tablet.

However, the decisive factor for this innovation was not just a simple idea, but on the one hand the associated development process and on the other the acceptance of a broad public.

The quality criterion "innovative" only applies to a product or a service if it actually appeals to a broad public and a corresponding change in our previous conventions is associated with it. On smartphones in particular, we can see how strongly this innovation has influenced our lives and, above all, the way we communicate with each other. For companies today, innovation is therefore a decisive factor in order to be successful on the market in the long term.

Numerous innovations of the last decades were not created by groundbreaking new technological developments, but by a new or fundamentally changed application of an existing technology. This also applies to the use of dominant technologies in a particular market segment.
The invention of the mountain bike can be seen as an example for the conquest of a new market segment. Here an off-road bicycle was developed using existing components (wide tires, suspension, cable brake) and a new frame geometry. In addition to technical development, however, the decisive factor for the predicate factor "innovation" is above all consumer acceptance and the associated creation of a new market segment.

Innovations can be very versatile: in terms of application technology, production technology, materials, function or form. This always involves a radical departure from previously used methods, materials, functions or forms.

Cooperation with designers is a decisive factor in the development of innovative products. Over time, designers have developed a very broad, multi-faceted spectrum of experience that represents a valuable addition to a company's in-house specialist knowledge. Technicians and designers can come up with new, innovative concepts and solutions through constructive criticism and mutual help.
The result of this is "social creativity", which puts joint problem-solving in the foreground. As tasks become increasingly complex, this strategy will have a great future. However, it places high demands not only on the professional qualifications, but even more on the human qualities of the team members. Simple things like: being able to listen, building trust, wanting to work together, practicing tolerance, etc. – these are important aspects of a fruitful working atmosphere shaped by personalities.

One of the leading design agencies, designaffairs, has considerable know-how in the development of innovative product solutions. For one of their customers, Siemens Healthineers, designaffairs designed a magnetic resonance imaging scanner and surprised with several product innovations:

The design and usability of the Siemens MRI devices were decisively optimized for the three main user groups: the innovative lighting concept on the front of the device optically opens the entrance of the device and demonstrably reduces the patient's anxiety. This saves time and prevents faulty shots. The clearly structured, approachable design of the MRI device radiates reliability and trust. The revised operating concept with a large touch display and symmetrical arrangement of the operating elements on both sides enables medical personnel to operate the system in an optimal and safe manner. The completely new cladding concept can be easily opened and maintained by just one person, so that service time and costs can be reduced.

Innovation is an indispensable process to be successful on the market!

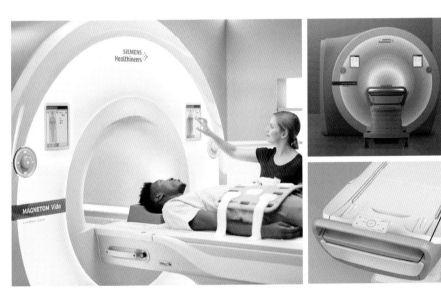

In this MRI from Siemens Healthcare, **innovation in the field of medical technology** is based, among other things, on material innovation. Comprehensive material research provided an innovative idea: where once the device casing used to be replaced at the cost of the manufacturer, now a special casing is used that can withstand the dynamic working environment without damage. The innovative lighting concept optically opens the funnel and demonstrably reduces the patient's anxiety.

Product: Siemens MAGNETOM Vida
Client: Siemens Healthcare GmbH
Design: designaffairs, Munich/Erlangen/Shanghai

Design provides advertising arguments

A convincing design attracts attention and is the driving force for communication. In times of digital media, the range of channels for advertising messages has increased enormously. Although classical advertising via print media and TV is still widespread, video channels (Youtube, Vimeo) or other social media offer new advertising channels that can be played on. Design without a targeted campaign is not easily accepted. Conversely, the communicative skills of design form a valuable potential for a modern advertising strategy. For example, at the launch of the KTM 1290 Super Duke, the motorcycle manufacturer KTM used only one medium, namely videos. In specially staged short films, the new models were staged with high-quality design and generated millions of clicks. Thus, even before the start of sales, a hype on digital platforms aroused desire. When using video portals and social media, it is thus possible to communicate much more directly, quickly and strongly with an interested group of buyers.

Another example of the skilful staging of design and innovation is the product launches introduced by Steve Jobs, which now take place at the Steve Jobs Theater in the heart of Apple Park. Never before in the history of industrial design has livestream attracted a worldwide audience and interested them in the presentation of the next model series and new products. Steve Jobs was a master of staging and the saying "One more thing..." accompanied him for over 20 years. In these lectures, design is the essential means to an end and, incidentally, an irreplaceable brand ambassador. Jony Ive, Apple's British chief designer, is also well known for his role as presenter, whose emotional video messages are communicated via the Apple website. This underlines the great importance that design has attached to the most valuable company (share value) on our planet.

When products receive a design award, there is also an advertising value associated with it. The resulting publicity (exhibitions, press releases, etc.) should not be underestimated. These awards can also be communicated via the product information.

Numerous industrial design bachelor and master theses generate videos, e.g., on the VIMEO video portal of FH JOANNEUM Industrial Design: https://vimeo.com/user63132342

Design makes quality tangible

There is a good chance of competing successfully on global markets especially for small and medium-sized enterprises with products of high technical quality. This high-tech quality must, however, be made visible first, which in turn is a primary task for product design. In many companies time and energy are, however, spent solely on technical development, leaving none for design. Outsiders are not aware of the huge effort going into technological development because they cannot tell from the neglected product form: it is underselling itself!

The designer's task is to make the existing inner qualities of the product outwardly perceptible. Possible options are the original, characteristic use of form and careful attention to details. We must, however, warn about misuse, such as taking the opposite approach and trying to enhance a technically inferior product with design. It may dazzle at first, but will not prove a successful strategy in the long term.

Design can cut costs

The opportunities for cutting costs with help of design lie in two areas: development costs and production costs. In the area of development, the holistic character of design in particular enables it to contribute to focused, efficient teamwork. The team can use its powers of representation to make new ideas – also from other members – more quickly visually available and discuss them more easily as a result. By showing alternative solutions in the form of graphic sketches, 3-D computer images or models, decisions can be made faster and more dependably, which can save additional costs in modeling.
Cutting production costs is a demand voiced throughout the entire design process: all the solution options have to be constantly monitored for their subsequent implementation costs. Can, for example, structurally identical parts be built and as a result tool costs be saved? Is cost-cutting modular design feasible?

With the help of a modular construction method costs can be saved quite simply. BÅS is a modular bathroom furniture system that does not require complex wall installations. A room concept with a multitude of individual elements that are formally inspired by nature.
Project: Odörfer "Bad der Zukunft" (Bath of the Future) in cooperation with Odörfer and Grohe
Design: Luis Meixner, Mara Pöllinger, Daniel Brunsteiner, FH JOANNEUM Industrial Design
Supervisors: Johannes Scherr (Design) and Gerald Steiner (Innovation), FH JOANNEUM Industrial Design

Design shapes the corporate image

A company's image can be understood as the reputation a company enjoys with outsiders. The means that lead to such a formation of opinion can be manifold. In a changing industrial culture, an increase in the product range and new forms of online trade, companies are striving to consciously shape their image. By means of suitable strategies and corresponding basic attitude of the management a corporate identity is developed. The **corporate identity** of a company requires a holistic view and an appropriate corporate culture or corporate philosophy.

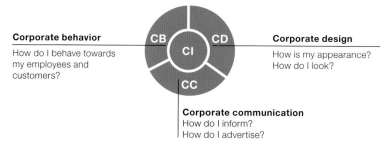

Corporate behavior

How do I behave towards my employees and customers?

Corporate design

How is my appearance?
How do I look?

Corporate communication
How do I inform?
How do I advertise?

The corporate identity consists of three areas:

1. Corporate design refers to the visual appearance and includes all design measures that characterize a company or institution. The corporate design should make a company appear as a unit and is therefore based on uniform constants in design such as company logo, stationery, employee appearance, packaging, advertising (print offline and web online), trade fair stand design through to company architecture. Product design is undisputedly of great importance because it is directly experienced by the customer. Corporate design supports the given goals of corporate identity, which are oriented towards values. Ethical principles such as responsibility for people and the environment, social commitment, etc. play a role here.

2. Corporate behavior is a kind of code of conduct. This refers to a company's internal behavior towards its employees, suppliers, etc. and its external behavior towards its customers, the public and their communication policy. Internal communication is defined as the style of leadership or the way employees interact with each other. The most important external communication is probably the consultation with the customer and the handling of complaints.

3. Corporate communication usually contains four different instruments: advertising, sales promotion, public relations and sponsoring (sports promotion or sweepstakes). Advertising is based on consistently applied design features such as logos, fonts, colors, etc. and a strategic overall concept that helps to increase the level of awareness or image of a company. All these activities are summarized in a corporate design manual. Companies like Olivetti and Braun have made important contributions to corporate culture in the past. A central element in the development of a corporate identity is insisting on the core messages of the corporate philosophy in order to increase recognition.

Design and brand

Products are strong brand ambassadors. Apart from customer service, there is no other way to get as closely in touch with a brand as with the product you are using. Brands themselves are abstract entities that are brought to life primarily through communication. This brand communication includes the values that the company embodies or wants to embody. These values can be very different. Some companies, for example, want to convey joy or freedom; others stand for sustainability or performance. Part of this communication is the design of the products. In the best case, the company's brand values should be experienced here, otherwise the "dazzling soap bubble" that was painstakingly created by brand communication may burst. The customer has certain expectations that have been awakened by this kind of communication. If these are not redeemed, disappointment arises, in the worst case rejection. In the best case, however, the buyer's expectations are exceeded. Then enthusiasm arises.
A designer should therefore always intensively concern himself with the values of the company for which he is designing the product and consider which creative means can be used to make them tangible. In addition to the subjective assessment by the experts of the development team, there is also the possibility of measuring the brand congruence of the designs using special methods. These are based on findings from analytical psychology, gestalt psychology, neuropsychology or perception psychology, such as the SimuPro® tool developed by designaffairs.

In the automotive industry, **corporate design** is an important instrument within the framework of a coherent corporate identity. The T-ONE project is the reinterpretation of the VW T-model for the year 2025, in which the DNA of the VW commercial vehicles such as variability, robustness, reliability and longevity was considered in the design concept. Current trends such as autonomous driving, urbanization, sharing concepts, etc. were included in the study.

Project: T-model – VW commercial vehicle 2025 in cooperation with Volkswagen commercial vehicles
Supervisors: Markus Rudlof and Zdenek Borysek, VW Design,
Michael Lanz, Marc Ischepp, Miltos Oliver Kountouras, FH JOANNEUM Industrial Design

What are the communication skills in design?

Design and functions

Preliminary remarks

One of the greatest problems for consumers is assessing product quality. This evaluation is mostly purely intuitive and tends to remain superficial. In addition, only partial aspects of the product are considered, which is why partial qualities are elevated to overall quality. Due to this unsatisfactory form of product assessment, various methods of product analysis have been developed.

To increase the objectiveness of the process, for example, scientific methods were introduced paving the way for the claim that "design has become measurable".

This claim is questionable, as a quotation by astronomer Rudolf Kühn shows: "If we take a tape with a recording of a Mozart symphony, I as a scientist can make any number of statements about it. I can weigh it, measure it, analyze the material, and determine its chemical composition. I can even count the vibrations preserved on it, plot the deflections on a graph – but I still have not recorded anything about the essence of the music that is also contained in same form in these plain facts. Natural science finds itself in a similar situation with regard to the world. What it says about the world may be correct, but is by no means everything; if it maintains it is everything, then it is wrong."[1]

It is clear that science alone is much too one-sided. What are the consequences? The answer can only be a holistic approach to the problem.

The model described below was developed on the basis of design theory work by Jochen Gros[2], Bernd Löbach[3] und Arnold Schürer[4].
It regards a **product as having various functions** which have an impact on people and the environment.
To illustrate this complex subject, "cutlery" is taken as an example several times in the description below.

Human-object-space relationships

A product must never be assessed in isolation. Therefore, the following relationships and interactions must be particularly taken into account:

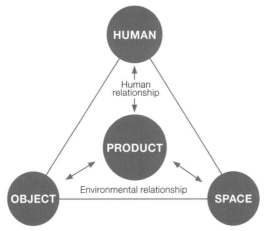

Human-object-space relationships

The **product-human relationship** (human relationship)

This relationship is experienced very quickly in the case of cutlery: we look at it, pick it up and put food in our mouths with it. Cutlery that looks good will please us, while a knife that does not cut well will annoy us.

The **product-object relationship** (close environmental relationship)

When the table is set, the cutlery is surrounded by many things: plates, glasses, napkins, bowls, tablecloth, etc. The table itself, chairs and lamps are naturally also to be included here, as well as the food and drinks.
The cutlery may be in harmony with all these surrounding objects or it may clash with them. (This may be the case, for example, if the cutlery looks big and heavy, while the china and glasses are thin and delicate.)

The **product-space relationship** (wide environmental relationship)

If we extend the idea of the surroundings, we go from the cutlery to the set table and then the room where the people will eat. Here, too, the relationships may be problem-free or critical. A large, lavishly decorated table will definitely not be set off to optimum effect, for example, in a low, narrow room. It would rather indicate that a desire for prestige is in conflict with the host's true social standing.

Function levels

Starting with a person, there are three relationship levels that form the basis for deriving the most important basic product functions.

The cutlery example can again be used to illustrate this point:
Imagine the following scenario: people that we have only recently met invite us for a meal. First of all we have an aperitif together and then they lead us into the dining room. We sit down, pick up the cutlery and start to eat. We therefore use the tableware. What do we notice in doing so?
We establish that the bowl of the spoon is too shallow to hold enough soup, the handle of the knife feels particularly good in our hands, but the prongs of the fork are so sharp that we could hurt ourselves on them.

We experience the physical aspects of the product at this **user level** and can therefore derive the **practical functions**.
First continuation of the cutlery example:
Once we have had something to eat, we can take a little rest and have a closer look at our surroundings. Gazing around, we will also turn to the cutlery. Now we will notice that the lines of the overall shape are pleasing to the eye, but the opulent decoration detracts from that elegance. The spoon and fork are well proportioned, but the knife handle does not look right with the blade.

We experience the sensory aspects of the product at this **observer level** and can therefore derive the **esthetic functions**.
Second continuation of the cutlery example:
Our hosts have just left the dining room to get the dessert. Alone again, we have the opportunity to explore new thoughts. Our gaze again falls on the cutlery, and we cannot explain why these simple, likeable people own such ostentatious tableware. Do they hope it will give them prestige? Or is it a family heirloom with sentimental value for them? The cutlery becomes a sign, a symbol for its owner.

We experience the social aspects of the product at this **owner level** and can therefore derive the **symbol functions**.

Let us summarize these derivations:

HUMAN		PRODUCT		FUNCTIONS
user level	▶	physical experiencer	▶	practical functions
observer level	▶	sensory experience	▶	esthetic functions
owner level	▶	social experience	▶	symbolic functions

These three basic functions of industrial products will have to be explained in more detail.

First of all, however, a few remarks about the **usage process**. It usually only relates to the practical function, and then only to the use of the product. A product can, however, also be used esthetically. This is the case, for example, when its shape is simply pleasing to look at and therefore gives pleasure (i.e., appearance or sensory function).

The usage can also be of a symbolic nature. Simply by owning and showing that you have fashionable products, you demonstrate to the environment that you are "in", that you "belong". This is therefore an extended concept of the usage process.[2] Before we analyze the usage process, we have to pose the fundamental question:

Do we actually need the product? Does the product make sense?

Given the prevalent market saturation, companies keep trying to create new needs in the consumer. An example: the subject of off-road vehicles alone is worth discussing. According to renowned automotive manufacturers surveys, 90 percent of all off-road vehicle owners never drive off road! What, then, drives people to such nonsense?

The answer can only be found in the associated symbol function: in the subconscious these cowcatcher are symbols of adventure, expeditions and far-off lands. At the same time people think that they are "customizing" the "mass-produced" off-road vehicle, i.e., giving it a personal touch.

There are countless products that merit the title of "affluent society" and often have unpleasant consequences, such as expensive loans, high repayment installments and personal debt.

Richard Sapper, an international award-winning designer, has put it in a nutshell:

"We should not be inventing even more objects that already exist and nobody needs, but ones that you need, yet do not exist."[5]

List of sources

(1) Wegeler R., o. A., lecture manuscript, Bregenz
(2) Gros, Jochen: Erweiterter Funktionalismus und empirische Ästhetik, diploma thesis, Brunswick, 1973
(3) Löbach, Bernd: Industrial Design – Grundlagen der Industrieproduktgestaltung, Munich, 1976
(4) Schürer, Arnold: Der Einfluß produktbestimmender Faktoren auf die Gestaltung, Bielefeld, 1974
(5) Brandes, Ute: Richard Sapper, Werkzeuge für das Leben, Göttingen, 1993

A product should be in use as much as possible throughout its life. This conserves resources, especially when devices are shared. **Swap sites** and **sharing communities** are enjoying growing popularity. A car is best used when it is in motion as much as possible and is not mainly parked in a car park or garage.

2. Choose "dirt scan"

4. Tool suggestion

1. Start app

3. Take photo of dirt

5. Find station

SHARING IS KÄRING is a rental system in the field of building cleaning and takes the trend "shareconomy" into account. The equipment station includes high-pressure cleaners, steam cleaners and wet/dry vacuum cleaners. A smartphone app provides advice on cleaning issues, shows where the next station is and enables the product required to be reserved.
Project work "Kärcher @ Smart Home" at FH JOANNEUM in cooperation with Kärcher.
Design: Dominik Krug and Rebecca Daum, FH JOANNEUM Industrial Design
Supervisors: Johannes Scherr (Design) and Georg Wagner (Engineering), FH JOANNEUM Industrial Design, Michael Meyer (Kärcher company)

Practical functions using the example of an organ transport system (donor heart):
The organ is kept alive by simulating blood circulation during transport. Compared to the original product (see below), the practical function of the transport has been significantly improved. The larger wheels and the optimized folding mechanism facilitate the transport and overcoming of obstacles. The interface was also redesigned and the usability optimized. The surfaces are as smooth as possible and therefore easy to clean.

Project: Master thesis at FH JOANNEUM Industrial Design in cooperation with SMAL GmbH
Design: Joscha Herold, Supervisor: Michael Lanz, FH JOANNEUM Industrial Design

The practical functions of the existing product have been profoundly further developed and improved.

Practical functions

When related to the practical functions, the usage process can be divided into five stages:

Acquisition
Transport
Storage
Use
Disposal

The first stage, **acquisition**, is mainly about gathering information. You want to gain an overview of the market, and as only some of the product characteristics are perceptible (evident, e.g., size, weight), you would like to learn more about the imperceptible ones (latent, e.g., product life).
Consumer organizations with their comparative product testing and such magazines as "Konsument" in Austria and "test" in Germany are ideal sources. These institutions are not influenced by any companies, and therefore provide neutral product information. They also examine product characteristics that buyers cannot gauge, such as material quality, corrosion resistance, safety, etc.

Transport can be of varying importance. If you only have to transport the product from the shop to the place where it will be used, this factor will play a comparatively minor role. It is, however, of much greater significance if the product is intended for travel use (e.g., a camera tripod or hairdryer).
If we go back to the cutlery example, the transport factor is not usually of any consequence. It does, however, play a significant role in camping cutlery, where such criteria as low weight and small volume are very important. In addition to these two, some other criteria also have to be taken into account: the protection of sensitive parts during transport (e.g., protective film on a shaver) and prevention of injury (e.g., knife, scissors).

The significance of the **storage** factor can also vary considerably. If chairs are used in a dining room in the home, storage will not be important. In a multi-purpose hall, on the other hand, where a lecture may be held one day and an exhibition the next, this factor does play a decisive role.

There are two possible solutions: folding or stacking chairs (and the transport factor is again at play here: how do you move a larger number of chairs?).
Or again using the cutlery example: delicate silver has to be stored much more carefully than hardwearing stainless steel cutlery. The storage factor is generally more important in the catering trade than in the home.

The actual core phase of the usage process, the **use**, is examined in more detail under the utility requirements described below.

We will therefore continue here with **disposal**. If in the course of a product's lifecycle it ceases to fulfill its basic function (e.g., because it is broken or worn out), cannot be repaired or has become outdated as much better technologies are on the market, it has to be disposed of. The best solution is eco-friendly recycling of the product that can no longer be used as opposed to dumping it on a landfill.

These **ecological aspects** have become increasingly important in view of our whole environment. They should therefore be taken into consideration from the very beginning, that is to say from manufacture through use to disposal of the product: "from cradle to grave".

Is it a burden on its environment during all these phases as a result of pollutants, noise, high energy and raw material consumption? Or is it an eco-friendly product that can be recycled? In relation to cutlery, for example, it is primarily a question of material selection (plastics that cannot be separated from metal or metal only), but also of clean production methods (e.g., emissions from plating baths, etc.). The ideal product does not have to be disposed of, but can always be returned to natural or technical uses: "from cradle to cradle".

During the usage process, demands are placed on the product, which we call **utility requirements**. The most important criteria of the practical function are listed below:

Usefulness

This should clarify whether a product really does fulfill the purpose for which it was developed. The basic function of cutlery, for example, is to enable you to divide food into bite-sized amounts and then place them in your mouth. This requires the cutlery to have suitable "tool characteristics", i.e., the knife must cut well, the spoon must be able to hold a certain amount of liquid, and the fork must be able to go through more solid food.

Controllability – handling

A very important area that also comes into ergonomics and usability studies. It is a case of adapting the work and therefore the tools to the users and not vice versa! Some interesting looking cutlery, for example, does not feel comfortable in your hand. You should therefore simulate the most important movements in the usage process before buying anything.

Safety

This is a demand that also applies for the duration of the entire usage process. In the case of cutlery, for example, fork prongs that are too sharp may lead to injuries while you are eating, and also pose a risk when you are cleaning, washing up or drying them. This point is rarely given due consideration, as can be seen from children's cutlery, for example, where it would be of particular importance.

Care – maintenance

To ensure that a utensil is always ready for use, it must be cared for properly. Most of us want this to involve as little work as possible. Is cutlery dishwasher safe or not? Will the wooden handle become rough and unsightly in time? How much care is needed for different materials, such as silver or stainless steel?

Durability – reparability

Reparability is essential to ensure extended service life. In general, it will depend on whether a wearing part can be replaced or whether housing is glued or screwed together. Labor costs are an additional factor: is repair worthwhile or would replacement be cheaper?

The following example will demonstrate what usage process and utility requirements mean in practice. A list of evaluation criteria for a vacuum cleaner's practical function could look like this:

1 Startup
(preparing the vacuum cleaner, plugging in the cord, switching on)

2 Cleaning smooth surfaces
(cleaning effect, time and effort required, maneuverability of the vacuum cleaner)

3 Cleaning smooth carpets
(cleaning effect, time and effort required, maneuverability of the vacuum cleaner)

4 Cleaning pile carpets
(cleaning effect, time and effort required, maneuverability of the vacuum cleaner)

5 Cleaning rugs
(cleaning effect, time and effort required, maneuverability of the vacuum cleaner)

6 Cleaning under low furniture
(accessibility, range, maneuverability)

7 Cleaning upholstered furniture
(accessibility)

8 Adjusting the vacuum cleaner
(changing the nozzles, different pile heights, suction power control)

9 Behavior in the working environment
(suction characteristics on various surfaces, pushing or pulling the appliance, furniture protection, radius, etc.)

10 Maintenance, hygiene
(changing the dust filter)

11 Operating noise
(at full/reduced power)

12 Sturdiness
(main appliance and attachments)

At this point we would like to address a problematic trend, namely the **short-term or disposable product**. It is now common knowledge that raw materials and energy are wasted unnecessarily. There is a danger that in the long term our behavior will be marked by this kind of waste. Since the 1950s there has been discussion about **"built in obsolescence"**, the expiration date built into products. This includes both technical obsolescence when the product or components fail, repair is too expensive and the product must therefore be discarded, as well as psychological or perceived obsolescence when changes in fashion lead to products being discarded as unfashionable even though they still function well. For the manufacturers it is supposedly desirable that their customers buy products, quickly throw them away and buy new ones again. For the users themselves and the environment, however, this is usually associated with negative consequences.

Take the following example from developmental psychology:
Children build relationships of varying intensity with their toys. If a favorite doll is damaged, its owner may demand that it be put back in one piece again. Such a treasured object needs to be repairable.
But the many products that are designed to be disposable or have a short life cannot be repaired. Depressing though it may be, the only option is to throw them away. Any attempt to patch them up is doomed to failure from the outset, depriving the child of an important learning process.

Children's toys must be built as robustly as possible and, above all, must be repairable. A Bobbycar is driven in use against cupboards or doors and should withstand these loads.

Children's furniture must meet children's needs in terms of product language and dimensions. Children's furniture series JAN; Design: Martin Prettenthaler FH JOANNEUM Industrial Design

Practical functions using the example of a kitchen island with modular worktops:
The central idea was to achieve an optimal workflow in order to make cooking easier, more efficient and more creative. The faucet is switched on and off by voice control. The lever regulates the water intensity and the slider controls the temperature – all with just one hand. An intelligent storage system helps to keep an eye on everything and to reduce or even avoid possible food waste.

Project: "SIEMENS Home Appliances Design Award", FH JOANNEUM Industrial Design in cooperation with BSH Hausgeräte GmbH
Design: Juliane Fischer, FH JOANNEUM Industrial Design, group work with Beatrice Schneider and Leon Rehage from the master program Interaction Design.
Supervisors: Ursula Tischner, Josef Gründler, Michael Lanz, FH JOANNEUM Industrial Design

The **product language** is determined by the target group and their needs!
Three muscle-powered micro-mobiles with supporting electric drive...

... for the target group of courier and delivery services in cities. Schaeffler Delivery is a robust load wheel for transporting goods in urban areas. Design: Paul Fally and René Stiegler

... for the "silver ager" target group (50plus) with an active lifestyle who appreciate a comfortable chassis. Schaeffler Silver Drive offers a lot of comfort (also in nature). Design: Simon Bildstein and Daniel Walch

... for the sporty commuter who gets to work fresh and sweatless and enjoys the bike highway after work. Schaeffler VARIED has two modes, "sporty" and "everyday". Design: Anna Lena Romeis and Christina Wolf

Project work micro-mobile at FH JOANNEUM in cooperation with Schaeffler AG.
Supervisors: Michael Lanz, Marc Ischepp, Miltos Oliver Kountouras, FH JOANNEUM Industrial Design

Product language

Jochen Gros[1] from the Hochschule für Gestaltung Offenbach, Germany, defines product language as the man-object relationships that are conveyed through our perception channels, our senses, i.e., as emotional product effects. He compares them with the practical functions that come about as a result of direct physical product effects. An example will make his definition clearer:

Imagine that we are standing in front of a door with a door handle. The practical functions of the door handle include the fact that the door actually opens when we press down the handle, that the handle is strong enough and does not break off when we apply pressure to it, that it is attached at an ergonomic height or that its size is suitable for use. Among the product language functions are the fact that we identify the lever on the door as a handle, that we trust in the reliability of the door handle (both as an opener and in relation to its durability), that we feel the handle is inviting or off-putting, and whether we expect an old room, a cellar or a modern studio behind the door.

Like any language, the product language functions require further structuring
in **grammar/form** (syntax) and **meaning/content** (semantics).

The grammatical aspects refer to the formal esthetic functions, i.e., the form elements of shape, color, material and surface, and the form structure between the poles of order and complexity.

The semantic aspects, also called signal functions, convey the meaning and are of particular interest. Here Gros distinguishes between **sign functions** and **symbol functions**.

To explain this, let us go back to our door handles:
An ergonomic looking handle is a sign of good handling, while a gold-plated surface is a symbol of affluence or ostentatious pretentiousness. We can derive from this that it is not about the isolated examination of object features, but about their effect on the observer.
These man-object relationships vary considerably. Signs relate directly to the product and its practical or technical function, and thus demand a certain behavior from the observer. Typical sign functions are the effect of stability, precision, orientation, endurance or flexibility. Symbols, on the other hand, do not relate directly to the product; they rather trigger cultural, social or historical associations. Typical symbolic functions are, e.g., luxury, modesty, eroticism, freedom, nostalgia, etc.

In practice the analysis of sign functions is not difficult, as one can check logically whether the practical or technical functions correspond to the product language.

Interpreting symbol functions is a far more complex procedure.

The sight of a Ferrari reawakens youthful dreams in one observer, while someone else will see it as a prime example of the Italian sense of form, and for others it is a symbol of today's rampant, aggressive materialism. Personal values and worldviews will color interpretation, reflecting our pluralistic society.

But it is also a reminder for us to look at things in a particularly careful, holistic way.

By combining the theory of product language[1] [2] [3] with the functional levels of a product shown above, we can derive the product functions in the model shown below.

List of sources

(1) Gros, Jochen: Grundlagen der Theorie der Produktsprache – Einführung, Offenbach, 1983
(2) Bürdek, Bernhard E.: Design: Geschichte, Theorie und Praxis der Produktgestaltung, Cologne, 1991
(3) Steffen, Dagmar: Design als Produktsprache, Basel/Berlin/Boston, 2000

PRODUCT FUNCTIONS AND FUNCTION LEVELS IN DESIGN

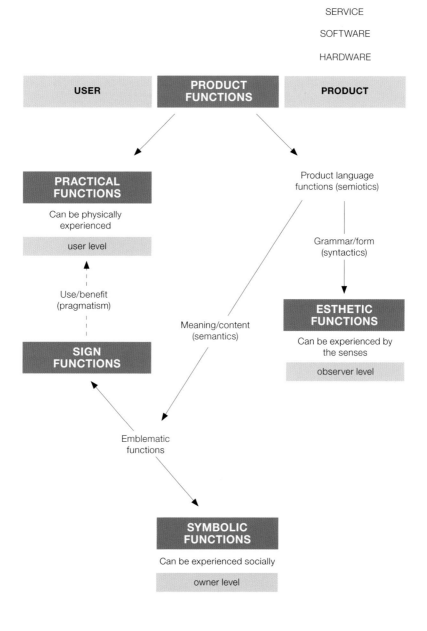

SERVICE

SOFTWARE

HARDWARE

| USER | PRODUCT FUNCTIONS | PRODUCT |

PRACTICAL FUNCTIONS

Can be physically experienced

user level

Product language functions (semiotics)

Grammar/form (syntactics)

Use/benefit (pragmatism)

Meaning/content (semantics)

ESTHETIC FUNCTIONS

Can be experienced by the senses

observer level

SIGN FUNCTIONS

Emblematic functions

SYMBOLIC FUNCTIONS

Can be experienced socially

owner level

Esthetic functions using the example of a tea maker:
The preparation and drinking of tea is something very sensual. The perceptible qualities of the product should also correspond to this: a glass body with balanced proportions and protection against the heat generated in the glass container. The aim of the project work was to develop innovative kitchen appliances for health-conscious nutrition.

Project: "Cooking 2.15", FH JOANNEUM Industrial Design in cooperation with Philips Austria GmbH
Design: Hannah Katzlberger, FH JOANNEUM Industrial Design
Supervisors: Johannes Scherr (Design), Georg Wagner (Engineering), FH JOANNEUM Industrial Design

Esthetic functions

In product language, the esthetic functions are assigned the role of "grammar", meaning they are therefore responsible for the formal aspects (syntax). Strictly speaking, we should call them formal esthetic functions (1), as we start out from a purely formal way of looking at things and consequently express the meaning of the content with the signal functions (product semantics). For the sake of simplicity, however, the abbreviated term "esthetic functions" is used here.

Esthetics is the study of **perceptible appearances** and perception by means of the human senses. The fundamental principles are too complicated to be discussed in full here.

A comprehensive evaluation requires that perception not be restricted to sight alone. Even though **visual perception** accounts for 70 to 80 percent of the information we take in, the importance of **smell, taste, hearing** and **touch** must not be underestimated.

Cutlery, for example, may cause loud background noise in combination with certain types of china, wooden handles feel warmer than metal ones, and inferior plastic handles can give off an unpleasant smell. When it comes to evaluating esthetic appearances, it is worth noting that the associated values and standards are influenced by social factors and can change over time, which affects above all color preferences and of course tastes in fashion and interior design.

The central concept in esthetics is **form**. The **elements of form** are shape, material, surface and color. Simply adding these elements together does not produce a form, but at best an amorphous conglomeration. For the creation of form, **structuring relationships** must exist between the **form elements**.

In this example, two or three randomly placed lines are turned into either a cross or a triangle once ordering principles have been applied. Thus the elements have taken on form.

Back to the form elements:

Form element			Ordering relationships	
2 lines	/ \	(amorphous)	+	(a cross)
3 lines	/ \ ▬	(amorphous)	△	(a triangle)

Shape

Because in most cases shape is the most important form element, in colloquial usage it is often equated with form. Shape quantity is distinct from shape quality. Shape quantity is basically the size of the product. Smaller cutlery creates a more modest, larger cutlery a more imposing impression. Shape quality is greatly determined by the **direction** of the shape. A **horizontal** orientation has a restful, stable effect, a **vertical** orientation looks active and important, but more unstable, while a **diagonal** orientation appears dynamic and exciting.

Subconsciously they evoke associations with a human figure: horizontal = lying passively; vertical = standing actively; diagonal = leaning forward to run.
The direction of the shape of a piece of cutlery may not be important, but the lines and the primary and secondary shapes are. The **lines** are determined by the shaping and can be soft and curved or hard and straight.
The **primary shape** may be geometric (e.g., cube, cylinder or sphere segment, or a combination of these) or organic.
The **secondary shapes** are the details that are worked into the primary shape, such as plastic, relief-like designs. A basic rule is that the stronger the secondary shapes, the weaker the effect of the primary shape. Excessive decoration can completely spoil the primary shape.

The question of **proportion** naturally plays an important role. In a knife, what is the ratio of blade length to blade width or of blade to handle? It affects the harmony. There are two basic kinds of proportions: the golden section and the modular system.
The **modular system** commonly used in the industrial age is based on a basic module of fixed dimensions. All the other units in the system must be a multiple of the basic module. The standard modular system used in the furniture industry is based on a basic module measuring 30 x 30 cm, which means that the individual units have widths and heights of 30, 60, 90 or 120 centimeters.

Modular system using the example of a sailing yacht. Project: "Yacht of the Future", FH JOANNEUM in cooperation with Sunbeam Yachts. Bachelor thesis by Johanna Königsberger, Lukas Wochinger
Supervisors: Lutz Kucher, Johannes Scherr, Michael Lanz, FH JOANNEUM Industrial Design

The **golden section**, or divine proportion, refers to the most harmonious ratio between two parts at around 2:3 (or to be precise 21:34).
The common paper size (DIN A 0, 1, 2, 3, 4 ...21:29.7) is perhaps the best-known example.

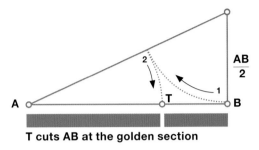

T cuts AB at the golden section

Golden section (constructive determination)

Surface

The surface finish can be perceived not only visually but touching, by touching it with your fingertips. Haptic perception means feeling something with your whole hand. The following effects are ascribed to various surfaces:

These associations are frequently put to use in cutlery, e.g., a matt handle or a shiny blade. Two-dimensional decoration can also be created with different surface finishes.

Material

This refers not to a material's technical properties, but to the sensory impressions that it creates. Wood is associated with warmth and good grip, while steel is identified with coldness and hardness. How the material is used is also important.
For example, does a chosen material do justice to the form and function of the cutlery? Plastic is perfectly acceptable for salad servers (resistant to acid), but not for cutlery because plastic is still not credited with sensory qualities. Nevertheless, imitation materials are highly popular. New materials and technologies can produce remarkably convincing copies of luxury materials.

PUMA NAO is an outdoor basketball shoe concept based on new production methods and **innovative materials**. The shoe consists of a rubber outsole that curves around the foot, an individually 3-D-printed insole, a woven, sock-like upper material and a lacing system made of a ribbon. The user can interact visually via interwoven "smart fabrics" and displays and read the current score or collected data on physical performance. The chip in the shoe contains a GPS and an acceleration sensor as well as batteries and a vibrator for haptic feedback. An app on the smartphone is linked to the shoe, allowing several players to network or organize games on the free field.

Project: Bachelor thesis at FH JOANNEUM Industrial Design
Design: Julian Loretz, FH JOANNEUM Industrial Design
Supervisors: Michael Lanz, Johannes Scherr, FH JOANNEUM and Tracy Goodsmith, Head of PUMA Sportstyle Footwear Design

In the course of evolution, materials and structures have developed in nature that can react to changing environmental conditions. Material scientists are increasingly investigating these biological systems in order to develop intelligent materials from them. These newly developed "smart materials", for example, have self-healing properties. This has the advantageous side effect that car paints can seal a scratch on their own. In car tires, rubber has been processed in such a way that cracks can close automatically without losing elasticity or stability.

Another example of the production of new materials would be the recycling of coffee grounds. The coffee residue is collected and used in a special process to produce coffee cups, which in turn protects our environment.

Color

Color psychology deals with the effects of different colors on people. This broad field can only be touched on briefly here, but the key point is that the stimulating effect of color on psyche and mood is very high. In product design a distinction is made between two main groups of colors: active, strong colors, which make the product stand out from its surroundings, and passive, neutral colors, which enable it to blend in with the background. Product size is relevant: bold colors are better suited to smaller objects, as they can make larger ones look garish and dominant.

In the case of cutlery, the relationship with the surroundings must be given careful thought. Should the tablecloth be colorful and the china and cutlery remain neutral? Or should the tablecloth be neutral and the cutlery highlighted with color? Should the colors be matching or complementary shades? The results may be harmonious, exciting, tense, quiet, boring, etc.

Color variations of the PUMA NAO, an outdoor basketball shoe concept.
Design: Julian Loretz, Bachelor thesis at FH JOANNEUM Industrial Design
Supervisors: Michael Lanz, Johannes Scherr, FH JOANNEUM and Tracy Goodsmith, Head of PUMA Sportstyle Footwear Design

This brings us to **form concepts**[2] and **form structure**.

In the **additive form concept**, individual elements are added together. The primary and secondary shapes look as if they have been joined together, but not combined.
In the case of the **integrative form concept**, the individual parts are not only put together, but also combined in terms of design. The secondary shapes are adapted to the primary shape.
The **integral form concept** goes even further by making the overall shape dominate, with all the other elements subordinate to it. The secondary shapes have become an integral part of the primary shape.

additive   integrative   integral

Design concept taking a bottle opener as an example

Complexity and order

These are the two most important phenomena in the relationship between the form elements of shape, material, surface and color, and form structure. They are mutually exclusive and act as poles with the tension of esthetic perception building up between them.

COMPLEXITY interesting, stimulating   ORDER pleasant, calming

LEICA Unique Moments by Elisabeth Schmeißl   LEICA V by Marta Matušin

Project: "Leica – Die Zukunft der Fotografie" (Leica – The Future of Photography), FH JOANNEUM in coope-ration with Leica Camera AG
Supervisors: Michael Lanz, Johannes Scherr, Gerald Steiner, FH JOANNEUM Industrial Design and Mark Shipard, Christoph Gredler, Leica Camera AG

Given that complexity is the opposite of order, it will suffice to list the key ordering principles:
– a horizontal-vertical relationship system or orthogonality;
– symmetry and
– rhythm

Symmetrically built and rhythmically breathing man standing vertically on the horizontal earth corresponds to these ordering principles, which have been around since primeval times.
The following **perception scale** is based on research by K. Alsleben and A. Moles[3]:

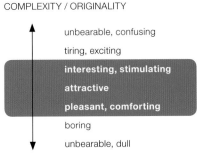

COMPLEXITY / ORIGINALITY

unbearable, confusing

tiring, exciting

interesting, stimulating

attractive

pleasant, comforting

boring

unbearable, dull

ORDER / BANALITY

The effects described on the scale show that there is a middle zone, which is of particular interest to perception. It is impossible to give an optimum value, as it also depends on subjective factors, such as the person's temperament and state of mind. The **optimum middle zone** on the perception scale has interesting parallels in behavioral research and motivation psychology[4]:

If there is too little or too much stimulation no life is generated. Similarly, the motivation to learn is substantially diminished by too high or too low a level of difficulty.

This scale can be applied both to the individual form elements and to the form as a whole. A highly ordered form with smooth surfaces but complex colors can give a balanced overall impression. To ensure holistic evaluation, the product should, if possible, not be examined in isolation; its surroundings should be included as far as human perception extends (scope of sight, hearing, tactility, etc.).

The law of compensation also holds true here: the more complex the environment, the more ordered the product should be (and vice versa): **the more complex the environment, the more ordered the product should be (and vice versa).**

List of sources:

(1) Steffen, Dagmar: Design als Produktsprache, Basel/Berlin/Boston, 2000
(2) Bürdek, Bernhard E.: Design: Geschichte, Theorie und Praxis der Produktgestaltung, Cologne, 1991
(3) Heufler, Gerhard/Rambousek, Friedrich: Produktgestaltung – Gebrauchsgut und Design, Vienna, 1978
(4) Kükelhaus, Hugo: Organismus und Technik, Frankfurt am Main, 1993

Product semantics

For many industrial design experts, product semantics[1], the symbolic functions of products, is a crucial focal point because it opens up interesting opportunities for a new quality of design. In addition to practical and esthetic functions, products clearly have meanings or symbolic characteristics. The effects of product semantics can easily be demonstrated. If one looks at a drill and sees it as rugged, powerful and long-lasting, as well as easy to operate and handle, then its most important properties are clearly expressed in the product language[2] and thus the design is also good in semantic terms. Rather than perceiving the symbols consciously, the user experiences the product in an intuitive, emotional way.

Or semantic qualities can be entirely lacking. Worse, the logical symbolism may be turned on its head. If a coffee machine, which by rights should be associated with a pleasurable ritual, exudes all the charm of sterile laboratory equipment, it is likely to disappoint the expectations of the users and their potential guests. Of course, those expectations can vary greatly. Does the target group live in Germany, Italy or Greece? The coffee-drinking habits in each of these countries are very different. This means that product semantics must focus not only on the interrelation between man and product but also on the cultural background, including social and emotional factors. It was a long time before this complex range of requirements was systematically addressed.

The Industrial Designers' Society of America (IDSA), headed by Klaus Krippendorf and Reinhard Butter, discussed product semantics at its annual conference for the first time in 1983. The results of the seminar filled a whole issue of the IDSA magazine, "Innovation". Designers were finally paying attention to an area that up till then had been the prerogative of communication science, psychology and sociology.

That same year Jochen Gros presented his "Fundamental principles of product language theory"[3] at the University of Art and Design in Offenbach. He extended the previous overly restrictive function concept to include the signal function, thus systematically incorporating the semantic aspects into the function structure for products.
Why did designers suddenly become so interested in product semantics? The reasons date back to trends that emerged in the 1960s and 1970s.

Uniformity

As global markets develop, regional uniqueness progressively goes by the board. Products become increasingly similar, often to the point where they are hardly distinguishable. Instead of being designed in a way that reflects identity, innovative product ideas are concealed behind unimaginative packaging.

Loss of identity

Predominantly mechanical products are easy to identify – a pair of scissors is recognizable as such – but the age of microelectronics has changed everything. Functionalism's motto of "form follows function" can no longer be applied. After all, who understands what goes on inside a chip?

Operation problems

The vast majority of users cannot keep up with increasingly complex and powerful technology and find many advances simply too daunting. From the experts' point of view microelectronics have brought incredible opportunities, but the average consumer has developed a fear of technology and inhibitions about using it.

The first response by designers came at the beginning of the 1980s. In Italy, the Memphis Group led by Ettore Sottsass sought to combat the sterile product environment with brightly colored, imaginative furniture, lighting and tableware. "New German design" followed suit, although here superficial gags predominated over serious ideas and the resulting media hype was out of proportion to the work produced. These designers failed to examine the issues of loss of identity, usability or forms in electronic devices. They produced one-off designs or expensive limited editions for collectors, and at the end of the day their work did little to advance our product culture. The examples given above illustrate that virtually any product can convey meaning. However, in one area product semantics has clearly prompted a search for new solutions and will continue to do so in the future: the interface between man and complex electronics.

Despite the fact that progressive miniaturization has expanded design freedom, for the most part technical innovations have not yet led to independent, understandable forms. New opportunities have arisen from the veritable explosion in products, but the main problem is how to make operation understandable to the user. Thick manuals are not the answer, what is needed is a product language that is self-explanatory.

Planning communication between man and machine is called interface design. This means that the design has to cover the software as well as the hardware. Product language also applies here: there is a grammatical part, which primarily concerns the programmer, and a semantic part, which the designer will have to address. This requires interdisciplinary knowledge, i.e., a combination of semantics, psychology, software ergonomics, software development and graphics.

Product language functions, and therefore product semantics, are always a question of communication. What is this process?

According to the Meyer-Eppler[4] **communication model** the basic modules are transmitter, signal and receiver.

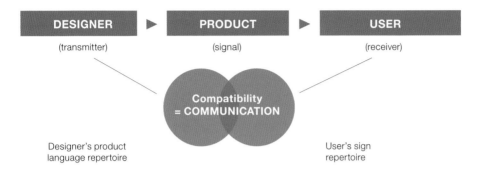

Design as a communication model

Communication is, however, only possible if the sign repertoires of a transmitter (designer) and a receiver (user) are compatible. The designers' task therefore has to be to translate a product's functions into signs that the receiver can also understand. This means that they have to study the target group closely and learn their "language" first of all.

List of sources:

(1) Bürdek, Bernhard E.: Design: Geschichte, Theorie und Praxis der Produktgestaltung, Cologne, 1991
(2) Steffen, Dagmar: Design als Produktsprache, Basel/Berlin/Boston, 2000
(3) Gros, Jochen: Grundlagen der Theorie der Produktsprache – Einführung, Offenbach, 1983
(4) Meyer-Eppler, Werner: Grundlagen und Anwendungen der Informationstheorie, Berlin, 1959

Product language functions using the example of a game:
"Participy" is a game for dementia patients and their relatives and is primarily intended to counteract loneliness and the associated accelerated cognitive decline of patients. This medium offers the caregivers an opportunity to penetrate through various game situations to the sick person and establish communication. The simple symbolic language and haptic experiences promote communication among patients, caregivers and relatives.

Project: Master thesis "Participy", FH JOANNEUM Industrial Design
Design: Alessandro Brandolisio, FH JOANNEUM Industrial Design
Supervisor: Michael Lanz, FH JOANNEUM Industrial Design

Indicator functions using the example of a multifunctional kitchen machine:
KÜMA 15 is the combination of a scale and a food processor. Despite the multi-functionality, the machine must still be user-friendly and self-explanatory. On the upper part, the "dry" and "liquid" ingredients can be weighed in two hoppers in order to avoid lump formation. The food is weighed in the food processor and added at the touch of a button, which prevents the ingredients from being decanted. After mixing the dough, the funnels and the mixing bowl can be removed and cleaned in the dishwasher. The connection of the two appliances saves space in the kitchen cabinet.

Project: "Home Heros" in cooperation with B/S/H Bosch and Siemens Hausgeräte GmbH
Design: Alexander Knorr, FH JOANNEUM Industrial Design
Supervisors: Johannes Scherr and Gerhard Heufler, FH JOANNEUM Industrial Design

Sign functions

In design, signs always relate to the practical functions of a product. They show its technical functions or explain its operation and handling. Sign functions therefore give direct information on the practical function (pragmatism). Here are a few simple examples of signs based on the work by Richard Fischer[1] und Berhard E. Bürdek[2] of Offenbach University of Art and Design:

Delimitation

Individual function areas, such as displays or controls, can be delimited within the overall form by means of outlining, raising or recessing, which makes them easier to distinguish.

Grouping

If there is a large number of identical elements, e.g., keys, perception and operation can be substantially improved by grouping them together.

Surface texture

Common example: if the surface of a housing is knurled, it is regarded as a sign for a gripping area.

Color contrasts

Using contrasts in color or brightness can also achieve structuring, grouping or signs for particularly important or dangerous elements (signal function).

Orientation

The orientation has to relate to the user in particular in many products, e.g., information terminals, remote controls or flashlights. This may affect the entire design concept.

Endurance

A solution is sometimes found for products that may ensure endurance in terms of structural design, but still not appear trustworthy visually to the user. In this case, the designer also has to demonstrate the actual endurance visually with suitable signs.

Stability

The same applies to stability as to endurance: a technically perfect solution may possibly appear too fragile to the observer/user. Signs of high stability are, for example, ribs (bracing or reinforcement).

Precision

Signs for precision are, for example, slenderness, sharp edges, perfect surfaces, clear lines and edges, and pronounced formal order.

Flexibility/variability

Movements in products can either be in stages or continuous, and take place in three directions: radial (e.g., pivot or hinge), axial (e.g., telescope or track) or radial spatial (e.g., ball-and-socket joint). The design should make these various movements perfectly clear to prevent incorrect operation.

Operation

The controls should clearly tell the user how to operate the device. Each control should therefore be designed so that it is also obvious whether it has to be turned, pressed or pushed. The whole operation procedure must be self-explanatory using suitable signs. This also includes the need for comprehensibility.

Comprehensibility

A glance must make a device's operating state immediately obvious and what alternatives are available. Greater use of microchips has gradually made it easier to give devices more and more functions. But it also requires comprehensibility to avoid confusion. The two examples below show that in the age of microelectronics in particular it is becoming increasingly important to use sign functions appropriately. This can substantially increase a product's utility value for consumers who have become confused by complex, intimidating technology.

List of sources:

(1) Fischer, Richard: Grundlagen einer Theorie der Produktsprache – Anzeichenfunktionen, Offenbach, 1984
(2) Bürdek, Bernhard E.: Design: Geschichte, Theorie und Praxis der Produktgestaltung, Cologne, 1991

Sign functions using a digital camera as an example:
Leica E is a new compact camera with two lenses. This allows you to work in 2-D mode and stereoscopic 3-D mode. The camera allows access to historical images and superimposition with real scenes. The displayed city map provides information about the selected location. The viewfinder can be rotated to the optimal position for shooting. The central circle on the display indicates the changeability/flexibility. Precision and high quality characterize the high product quality.

Project: "Leica – Die Zukunft der Fotografie" (Leica – The Future of Photography), FH JOANNEUM Industrial Design in cooperation with Leica Camera AG
Design: Miroslav Truben, FH JOANNEUM Industrial Design
Supervisors: Michael Lanz, Johannes Scherr, Gerald Steiner, FH JOANNEUM Industrial Design and Mark Shipard, Christoph Gredler, Leica Camera AG

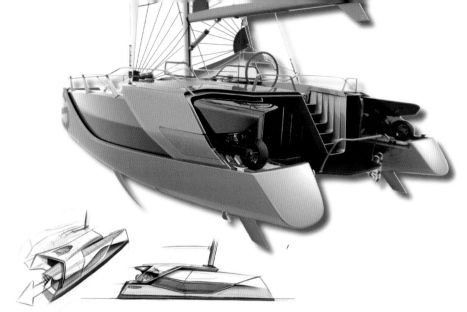

Symbol functions using the example of a yacht with integrated motorcycles:
Yachts are among the most prestigious objects, as they can be admired and compared in close proximity in the harbor. This catamaran offers an integrated storage and charging facility for two electric motorcycles. The Central European area has not only the most beautiful sailing areas, but also fantastic coastal roads and mountain passes. A perfect base for a dream holiday that combines the elegance of sailing with the passion and adrenaline of motorcycling. The electric motorcycles have a range of 400 kilometers. The design of the project is based on the emotions and dynamics of sailing.

Project: "Yacht der Zukunft" (Yacht of the Future), FH JOANNEUM in cooperation with Sunbeam Yachts
Bachelor thesis by Anja Didrichsons and Maximilian Troicher, FH JOANNEUM Industrial Design
Supervisors: Lutz Kucher, Johannes Scherr, Michael Lanz, FH JOANNEUM Industrial Design

Symbol functions

The symbol functions rank as one of the most complex areas of product language and can only be objectified to a limited extent. Their significance to design theory was not recognized until the 1980s.[1][2]

In the 1920s, the heyday of functionalism, the design dictum was **"form follows function"** – coined by American architect Louis Sullivan. Unlike Sullivan, the functionalists reduced "function" to mean the practical or technical one, but did not take in symbolic function.
This one-sided functionalism also came in for harsh criticisms and led to counter-reactions in the 1950s and 1960s, as it was often considered unemotional and boringly practical.

In the 1980s the original "form follows **function**" first became:
"form follows **emotion**", and finally: "form follows **fun**".

As so often in the history of design, the pendulum swung in the other direction. The new versions of the motto also fall short of the mark: they now deny the practical functions in many cases, instead of the symbolic ones.

In the interests of a holistic approach, it would be better to use the extended concept of functionalism formulated by Jochen Gros in the 1970s: "form follows function". This would not only mean the technical, practical functions, but also the symbol and sign functions!

The discussion could naturally be taken further: philosopher Andreas Dorschel rightly states that form is neither determined by function nor logically follows from it. His book "Gestaltung – Zur Ästhetik des Brauchbaren" (Design – on the Esthetics of the Useful)[3] examines these complex, theoretical relationships in an easily understandable form.

After this brief digression, let us return to the symbol functions, which we have assigned to the owner level, as they can be experienced socially. The product acts as a sign and, given its symbol character, is identified with the owner.

An example: a Rolls-Royce is instantly associated with affluence – even if its owner is not there – and this characteristic is also transferred to the owner. The symbol functions are indirect indications of sociocultural backgrounds, unlike the sign functions, which are direct indications of the practical functions.

Interpreting the relevant sociocultural relationships correctly is a difficult task and we will therefore structure it.

On the basis of work by Gert Selle (4), we will examine them on three different levels: cultural, social and personal. The product has an effect on all three levels as a result of its symbolism.

Zeitgeist – relevance (cultural level)

We are all members of today's society and therefore also part of our civilization and culture. Naturally, we can agree with this fact, question it or reject it, but we cannot escape from its presence or influence.

Group membership – status (social level)

Everyone feels the need to be accepted within his or her social group. This gives them a certain status and a certain sense of security. This status can be symbolized with products typical for the group. We therefore talk about **status symbols**.

On the other hand, people tend to aspire to higher social standing. They imitate their idols behavior, language, and clothing, also by using "their" products. A **prestige object** is therefore a product that symbolizes or emulates an ideal status. A Rolls-Royce, for example, is a status symbol for an oil sheik, but a prestige object for a sawmill owner.

Emotional ties – object association (personal level)

On this level there are often very close associations with an object that sometimes can only be explained by the relevant person's memories and personal experience. While the emotional bonds were usually very close with handcrafted (unique) objects, emotional ties and therefore object association is seldom possible in the case of today's mass-produced products. Emotional ties can sometimes be strengthened, for example, by changing or labeling the product, which makes the consumer's identity more pronounced in relation to the product environment. It then becomes "his" product.

Swatch opted for a highly successful approach in commercial terms in response to the demand for individualization. The company keeps the tool-intensive and therefore expensive engineering modules in use for a relatively long time, but changes the cheap colors, patterns and surface finishes at frequent intervals. Several collections are presented a year, often even in limited editions. This successful marketing strategy has often been imitated in the interim and has even been given a name: "swatchization". Closely connected with this development is the concept of "fashion".

By fashion we mean the short-term, periodic change of the external features of a society's members (and therefore also of their products).

Two basic needs determine the essence of fashion: on the one hand, the desire for **conformity**, i.e., people prefer design ideals that are accepted within their own social group.

And on the other hand, there is a need for **distinction**. People want to be different from other groups or the masses and seek individuality.

Here product usage can serve very effectively as a means of self-presentation, although suggestive advertising and the fashion dictates that often result can cause intended self-presentation to become self-deception.

Motorcycles are very well suited to signal group membership as a status symbol. In organized group trips you can experience a high feeling of freedom, which is permanently noticeable through the dynamics of the airstream. Motorcycles convey a good mixture of power, dynamics and high-quality technology in their product language.
Project: "Yacht of the Future", FH JOANNEUM in cooperation with Sunbeam Yachts
Bachelor thesis by Anja Didrichsons and Maximilian Troicher
Supervisors: Lutz Kucher, Johannes Scherr, Michael Lanz, FH JOANNEUM Industrial Design
(see also page 80)

List of sources:

(1) Gros, Jochen: Grundlagen einer Theorie der Produktsprache – Symbolfunktionen, Offenbach, 1987
(2) Bürdek, Bernhard E.: Design: Geschichte, Theorie und Praxis der Produktgestaltung, Cologne, 1991
(3) Dorschel, Andreas: Gestaltung – Zur Ästhetik des Brauchbaren, Heidelberg, 2003
(4) Selle, Gert: Produktkultur und Identität, in: form, No. 88, Seeheim, 1979

Mood boards

The changes in fashion trends, which are also becoming more and more rapid in the field of product design (retro look, new wave, etc.), or their juxtaposition and mix have led to many consumers becoming confused more and more frequently. Especially when products constitute a long-term, cast-intensive purchase, fashionable design means that they will soon appear outdated and should therefore be regarded critically. It is usually a case of styling in the sense of window dressing to boost flagging sales.

If the symbol functions are to be used correctly, they have to be oriented to the target group as well as possible. When defining a target group, it is no longer a case of class membership in the traditional sense, but a sense of belonging to a group with the same interests, activities and opinions in today's "patchwork" society. A highly successful tool in defining the target group is a **mood board**.

These collages of pictures are used to capture the mood of a target group: What are they like? What do they read? What do they wear? How do they spend their leisure time? What products do they buy? Answering these questions in the form of mood boards yields important conclusions about the world of values and is therefore extremely helpful for developing a target group-oriented product language.

TARGET GROUP

TRENDS FOOTWEAR BASKETBALL

Target group analysis and trend research on the subject of basketball shoes

Product analysis

To conclude this chapter on design from the consumer's point of view, we wish to point out that product analysis can also be carried out. This consists of function analysis and cost analysis. The **function analysis** covers all the functions mentioned in this chapter from the practical to the symbolic. This may become more understandable in another example.

Example: timer
Practical function – user level

1 Positioning (standing, hanging, carrying it around)
2 Setting/winding (turning resistance, one/two hand, assignment of hand/scale)
3 Visual reading (close/distant)
4 Audio signal (duration, volume, sound)
5 Cleaning (frequency, degree of difficulty)
6 Accuracy (at 5 min/60 min)
7 Ruggedness (fatigue strength, resistance to corrosion and breakage)

Esthetic function – observer level

1 Form quality (proportions, size)
2 Material selected (warm/cold to the touch)
3 Tactile properties (smooth/textured surface)
4 Color used (signal/restrained effect)
5 Overall visual impression (pleasant/unpleasant/unbalanced)

Sign function

1 Stability
2 Precision
3 Movement
4 Self-explanation of the operating process

Symbolic function – owner level

1 Relevance to present day (modern/nostalgic)
2 Group membership (target group relationship)

Let us now briefly turn to **cost analysis**. The utility value of a product having been determined during the function analysis, the exchange value is ascertained in the cost analysis. We are therefore on the buyer level as it were and can talk about an economic function. Consequently, the purchase price, running costs and resale value are determined. This part of product analysis does not present any problems, as all the factors can be assessed in figures.

Purchase price

Although the utility value may be identical, the cost prices of consumer goods can vary considerably. There are differences in the price of one and the same product, depending on how the various dealers do their costing. Neutral test reports have, however, shown that the most expensive are not necessarily the best! Here all you can do is collect as much information as possible and compare.

Running costs

The running costs tend to be ignored in estimates. They are also frequently underestimated in certain product groups, such as color printers. The initial purchase is surprisingly cheap, but the running costs are far too expensive (color ink cartridges) and the overheads get out of hand.

Resale value

The resale value also depends to a great extent on the product category. It can easily be calculated for vehicles, but is usually inflationary on the other hand in the case of, say, computers. Having discussed the most important points in cost analysis, we can derive the following procedure for a holistic product analysis from the consumer's point of view.

First of all the criteria must be adjusted to suit the relevant subject:
1. Collecting the criteria
2. Structuring or ordering according to function relationships and areas
3. Evaluating or weighting the criteria

Evaluating the function areas and criteria firstly serves the purpose of reducing the list of criteria to a sensible length (i.e., insignificant criteria have to be eliminated to improve the drawn up), which is much clearer and more meaningful than any points system. It provides accurate information as to the consumer's expectations of the product. What is decisive for the profile's accuracy is that it is determined by selected test subjects representing the target group.

Assessing the test objects

Every test object should be described before analysis: purpose, target group, material, size, special features, price, etc., but without rating it. This trains perception and makes the object more familiar. Then the actual evaluation can follow. Two different procedures are possible: either each product is examined individually using the complete criteria list, or all the products are examined and compared on the basis of only one criterion (cross-comparison). The latter approach involves specific examination of certain aspects of the whole product. To combine the partial evaluations in an overall assessment, the results are shown in a feature profile.

This method produces a quickly comprehensible overview of the most important product features, while a points system is only suitable for more detailed information on one area. Where the requirement and feature profiles correspond to the greatest extent, the highest product quality is achieved.

Product analysis of a toothbrush

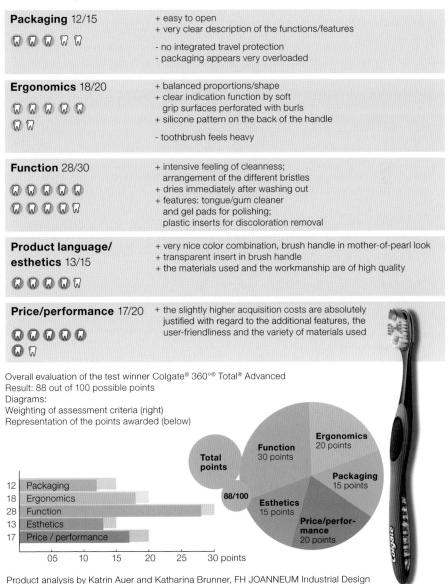

Packaging 12/15

+ easy to open
+ very clear description of the functions/features

- no integrated travel protection
- packaging appears very overloaded

Ergonomics 18/20

+ balanced proportions/shape
+ clear indication function by soft grip surfaces perforated with burls
+ silicone pattern on the back of the handle

- toothbrush feels heavy

Function 28/30

+ intensive feeling of cleanness; arrangement of the different bristles
+ dries immediately after washing out
+ features: tongue/gum cleaner and gel pads for polishing; plastic inserts for discoloration removal

Product language/ esthetics 13/15

+ very nice color combination, brush handle in mother-of-pearl look
+ transparent insert in brush handle
+ the materials used and the workmanship are of high quality

Price/performance 17/20

+ the slightly higher acquisition costs are absolutely justified with regard to the additional features, the user-friendliness and the variety of materials used

Overall evaluation of the test winner Colgate® 360°® Total® Advanced
Result: 88 out of 100 possible points
Diagrams:
Weighting of assessment criteria (right)
Representation of the points awarded (below)

Total points

Function
30 points

Ergonomics
20 points

Packaging
15 points

Esthetics
15 points

Price/perfor-
mance
20 points

88/100

12	Packaging	
18	Ergonomics	
28	Function	
13	Esthetics	
17	Price / performance	

05   10   15   20   25   30 points

Product analysis by Katrin Auer and Katharina Brunner, FH JOANNEUM Industrial Design
Supervisor: Michael Lanz, lecture "Design Basics", FH JOANNEUM Industrial Design

Ergonomics in product design

by Dr. Matthias Götz

Ergonomics in industrial design pursues the concept of user-friendly utility articles with the aim of optimizing the comprehensibility, manageability and comfort of consumer and investment goods. Ergonomics originated in the middle of the 19th century, when it was a matter of developing design rules to reduce the strain on people at work. Many of the insights gained from this time form the basis for product ergonomics, which is understood as a sub-area of ergonomics.

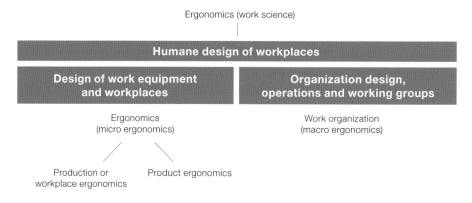

Ergonomics and its subareas according to Luczak et al. 1987[1]

The rules of ergonomics are so universal that we encounter them everywhere, at work as well as in our private lives. The same design rules apply to a private kitchen workstation as to a laboratory workstation. Comparable ergonomic criteria can also be used for the development of a clinical measuring device and a hi-fi full amplifier. Some areas have specialized, such as aerospace systems, human-product interaction in vehicles or the design of products and spaces for users with physical disabilities. For product ergonomics, a user unknown as an individual is significant, which requires the consideration of the large range of human characteristics and abilities.

The ergonomic design principles briefly described below must be integrated into the design process.

Anthropometric design

Anthropometry is the study of the dimensions, proportions and measurement of the human body (body dimensions, movement, weights, forces). The results of the measurements are summarized in tables, which form the basis of the anthropometric design.

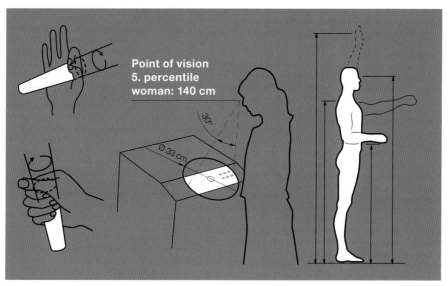

Dimensions and proportions of human beings

Lengths and distances of the extremities are considered as well as circumferences, areas and volumes. We learn, for example, diameters and lengths for optimum handle dimensioning.
A distinction is made between age, sex and also region, because depending on a person's origin, their height can vary considerably. The time at which the measurement data is recorded must also be taken into account, as people have become one to two centimeters taller in recent decades.
The design should apply to as large a proportion of the population as possible. For an office swivel chair, this means that it can be used by both very small and very large people, which requires the integration of height adjustability.

As part of the student project work for the conception of a medical laboratory device, the dimensions for the eye level of tall and short people standing are required in order to optimally design the display tilt angle and the font size of the display: when reading, care should be taken to minimize reflections and light reflections. Large people, who have the greatest reading distance with a table-top device, should be able to recognize symbols and writing without restriction.

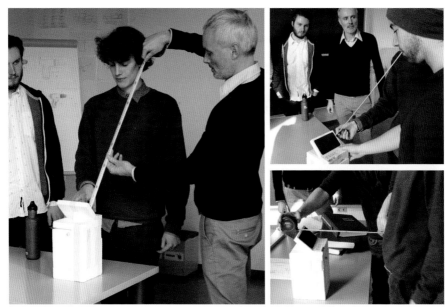

Spatial orientation of a touch screen for a medical laboratory apparatus

Visual perception

Considering the laws of visual perception enables the designer to use the form and graphics of a product to convey information in a targeted manner and also to control eye movements, which is a decisive contribution to the self-explanatory ability of a product or its intuitive handling; especially since the first interaction with a product is often eye contact, after which decisions about further actions are made.

In addition, selected color and light-dark contrasts as well as defined font sizes depending on the reading distance make a contribution to ensuring that a product is visually correctly perceptible and thus support optimum reading of advertisements.

For persons with a red-green visual impairment, for example, unrestricted reading is made possible by avoiding certain color contrasts, which corresponds to a barrier-free design.

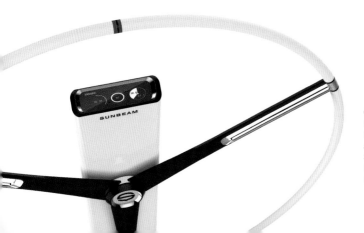

Control element sailing yacht.
Project: "Yacht of the Future"
Design: Johanna Königsberger and Lukas Wochinger
Supervisors: Michael Lanz, Lutz Kucher, Johannes Scherr, FH JOANNEUM

Photorealistic representation of the driver's cab of a sailing yacht

Knowledge about the basics of seeing and the functionality of visual perception of space have made virtual environments possible in the first place.
These virtual environments are not only used for testing and presenting product concepts, but are also part of products today, for example, when we think of data glasses.

Haptic design

Man has the ability to haptically explore an object with regard to its shape (size, contour, texture, weight, etc.). He also recognizes the movement possibilities of this object in space. By including this characteristic in the design, differentiated information can be conveyed.
For example, the form coding of actuators can be used to identify function groups. In addition to the differentiation from the other keys, a pressure switch with finger recess for "switching on and off", for example, allows operation by blind people or people with impaired vision.

Form-coded controls on a kitchen machine with weighing function.
Project work "Cooking 2.15" in cooperation with Philips Austria.
Design: Alexander Knorr, FH JOANNEUM
Supervisors: Johannes Scherr and Matthias Götz, FH JOANNEUM Industrial Design.

The appropriate choice of the surface material and its texture influences the qualitative appearance of a product. A satined metal surface is clearly distinguishable from a polished plastic surface with regard to its temperature and the static friction between material and skin and is perceived as being of higher quality.

The perceived feeling between the actuation travel and the forces occurring when moving controls, flaps, doors or pushers on products is described by the contents of the actuation haptics. A product can thus be given a desired haptic character, which conveys corresponding information and qualitative properties. The noticeable engagement of a door latch gives the user additional important feedback that the door is closed.

Acoustic design

The acoustic shape of a product is influenced by the choice of materials and their basic structure. A hollow metal case produces a different sound than an aluminum die-cast construction. In principle, it is important to avoid noises that negatively affect the quality of a product. Certain sound levels must not be exceeded in order to prevent damage to hearing and not to impair concentrated work in, for example, office environments.

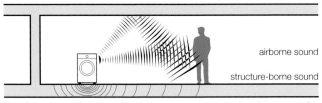

airborne sound

structure-borne sound

Sound development on a machine (airborne sound and structure-borne sound)

On the other hand, a noise can also be an important information channel that contributes to the understanding of an operating procedure. For example, a conventional touch screen has neither an acoustic nor a haptic feedback, as opposed to a mechanically locking knob, where clicking confirms the successful selection of a function. Acoustic signals are also frequently used to indicate errors or warnings.

In addition, a sound can also become an image carrier that can be clearly assigned to a trademark.

Information technology design

Information technology design aims to define the interaction between people and products, taking into account people's cognitive abilities. When handling a product, the human being absorbs information via his senses, processes it depending on his knowledge and experience and finally makes a decision after which he triggers an operating step (information conversion). When a product is used, the structural image of the human-product system describes the process of information transformation.

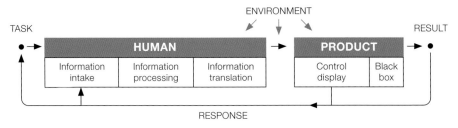

Human-product system based on Bubb1992[2]

The connection between the task and the fulfillment of the task (result) is defined by the human-product system. By intentionally influencing a product, the human being tries to correspond to a task set from the outside or by himself. Displays and operating elements represent the interface to the product, for which ergonomics provides extensive design recommendations. Operating sequences can thus be displayed logically and consistently. An overstrain of the human being by functional overload can therefore be controlled. The consideration of so-called inner models, i.e., knowledge based on experience, training and education, contributes to intuitive operation. It is generally assumed, for example, that the movement of a control unit "to the right, forwards" or "clockwise rotation" of the object when viewed from the operator causes it to switch on or increase; a movement "to the left, backwards" or "counter-clockwise rotation" causes it to switch off or decrease.

By providing feedback to humans, the machine contributes to interaction: the information about the fulfillment of the task and its comparison with the setting of the task allow the person to control the success of the work. Due to this comparison, it may be necessary to intervene in the work process again or to take corrective action. The feedback has to take place in a certain time window and can be transmitted via different sensory channels. In order to make systems particularly safe, it makes sense to address several sensory channels simultaneously, for example, to support a visual signal with an acoustic signal. The environment (e.g., sound, lighting) can have an influence on this structure of effects and must therefore also be taken into account in the design. In many cases – especially with electronic devices – the controls and displays are the only area in which a human-object relationship still comes about (aspect "black box", Bürdek 1992[3]), whereby their ergonomic design plays an increasingly important role.

Ergonomics workshop: development of cooktop scenarios with temperature and time control. Testing of different cooktop scenarios on a scale of 1:1.

During the ergonomics workshop in the third semester, students are given the task of developing cooktop scenarios. The first step is to design a self-explanatory operating concept for the temperature control. Then a group of cooking zones is to be arranged within a cooking field in such a way that each cooking zone can be clearly assigned a control element with display, everything can be read despite the presence of pans and pots, and the user does not burn his fingers in the process.

Integration of ergonomic design into the design process

Ergonomic design must be included in the design process right from the start, i.e., already in the research and analysis phase. Design recommendations in the form of standards, regulations and tables, which take human abilities and properties into account, help to check an idea and, if necessary, also to expand it, and provide decisive indications of the possible components, properties and necessary functionalities of a future product. The idea for a new product can be based on ergonomic findings.

If there are no rules for certain topics, it is advisable to carry out tests with test persons or ergonomic experiments in order to determine them.

The decision making process during conception and design is supported by the use of ergonomic checklists. 3-D human models can be used for the evaluation of digital product concepts. The number of prototypes actually built can thus be reduced.

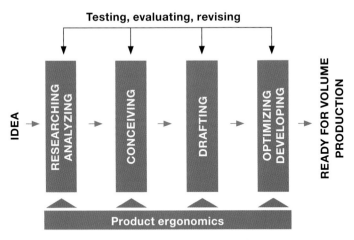

Integration of product ergonomics based on the design process according to Gerhard Heufler

Ergonomics is thus an element of the design process and is of course also continuously involved in testing, evaluation and revision in the individual process stages.

Lecture "Project work design & ergonomics"

Design process with focus on ergonomics
Project work "Tooltime" at FH JOANNEUM Industrial Design
Design: Tim Hinderhofer
The design study "Fein EBS300" by Tim Hinderhofer is an innovative interpretation of the classic hacksaw with optimized handling.

Historical example of a hacksaw (left), design by Tim Hinderhofer (right)

Package and features

Two saw blades moving in opposite directions are the basic technical principle of this hacksaw. A rechargeable battery provides the required energy. Thanks to two counter-rotating oscillating saw blades, a slight pressure from above is sufficient to saw, thus eliminating the horizontal movement control of the saw and allowing the operator to concentrate primarily on vertical cutting. The electrically driven saw blades ensure energy-saving cutting overall.

When designing the handle, care must be taken to ensure that both people with small and large hands can handle the saw optimally. For the handle cross-section, this means creating a wrap-around handle for a small hand that also allows sufficient space for the finger length of a large hand. A rectangular cross-section is suitable for this purpose. The length of the handle is again to be designed for a large hand, since even a small hand will find enough space on it.

A form-fit handle shape with finger recesses, which positions each individual finger, was deliberately omitted. The anthropometric characteristics of the hand differ so strongly from person to person that a handle segmentation suitable for an individual would lead to forced postures in the majority of users. A flat handle surface, which allows free positioning of the fingers, is therefore an advantage. However, the optimal spatial orientation of these handles is only suitable for right-handed persons. In order to do justice to all users, one needs an additional left-handed variant.

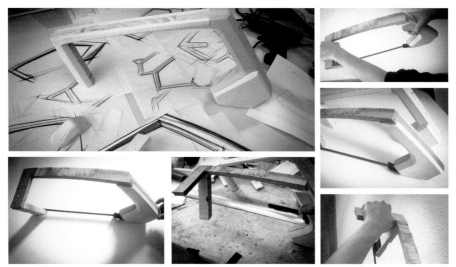
Ergonomics models for checking anthropometric design. Design: Tim Hinderhofer, FH JOANNEUM

The ergonomic data determined from tables were checked in several ergonomics models. With the aim of matching the functional axes of the saw to the axes of the hand-arm system, the spatial orientation of the handles was varied.

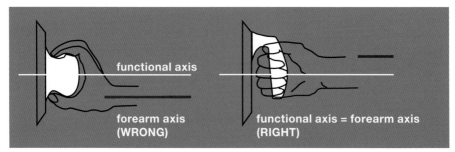
Assignment of functional and anatomical axes (HdE 2011)[4]

Translatory movements are better than rotary ones for coping with heavy working resistances. Translatory movements of the hand-arm system allow the use of large muscle groups with good body support. Anatomically speaking, this means that the longitudinal axis of the forearm must be aligned with the third metacarpal bone of the hand for ergonomic handle design.

The asymmetrical shape of the frame allows a clear view of the cutting area and therefore better control of the cutting process. A display shows the deviation from the vertical alignment of the saw blades and thus supports a vertical cut. The font size and line width of the display was designed to match the reading distance during use of the saw.

The hacksaw in use (top and bottom left) and working on the design model (bottom right) by Tim Hinderhofer, FH JOANNEUM Industrial Design

The basic shape of the saw and the clearly displayed handle positions are based on the familiar image of a hacksaw. The display concept as well as the control element design in the form of a push-button are self-explanatory and correspond to the familiar inner constructs of the human being. Thus both the cognitive abilities and the expectations of the person are taken into account.

Display of the vertical alignment of the saw and work on the design model (right)

List of sources:

(1) Luczak, Holger/Volpert, W./Raithel, A./Shwier, W.: Arbeitswissenschaftliche Kerndefinition, Gegenstandskatalog, Forschungsgebiete, Edingen-Neckarsulm, RKW, 1987
(2) Bubb, Heiner/Seifert, R.: Struktur des MMS; in: Bubb, Heiner (ed.), Menschliche Zuverlässigkeit, Landsberg, ecomed – Fachverlag, 1992
(3) Bürdek, Bernhard E.: Design: Geschichte, Theorie u. Praxis der Produktgestaltung, DuMont Buchverlag, Cologne, 1992
(4) Bundesamt für Wehrtechnik und Beschaffung, Handbuch der Ergonomie, 2011

How is a product created?

Design as a process

Preliminary remarks on the design process

Product development and the associated design process are subject to a constant renewal process. The tools created in the course of digitalization open up innovative design possibilities for designers. For example, the electronic drawing tablet or parametric design (with Grasshopper 3D) has already been used widely. These new tools influence the type of design not only in the manufacture of products, but also in the design process.

The goal of every design process is without doubt a high-quality and well thought-out product, system, service or user experience!

The task of the following chapter is to make the design process transparent and to introduce corresponding tools in design. A structured sequence of work steps sets the direction and shows how work is done in every design process. Each designer must discover the tools and methods used for himself and apply them as playfully as possible. At the outset, however, we would like to make some fundamental considerations and answer the question: What is good design?

In the 1970s **Dieter Rams** formulated **ten theses** on the **subject of design**, which were decisive for him and his colleagues at Braun Design. These principles, a kind of philosophy of design, served as an aid to orientation and understanding. But they should not and cannot be a commitment. The notions of what good design is have naturally evolved – just as technology and culture continue to evolve. Nevertheless, some theses have a universal character, especially at a time when topics such as resource conservation and user-friendliness are of great importance in the social debate.

1 Good design is innovative
The possibilities for innovation are not, by any means, exhausted. Technological development is always offering new opportunities for innovative design. But innovative design always develops in tandem with innovative technology, and can never be an end in itself.

2 Good design makes a product useful
A product is bought to be used. It has to satisfy certain criteria, not only functional, but also psychological and esthetic. Good design emphasizes the usefulness of a product whilst disregarding anything that could possibly detract from it.

3 Good design is esthetic
The esthetic quality of a product – and thus its fascination – is an integral aspect of its usability. Because it is certainly unpleasant and tedious to deal day after day with products that are confusing, that literally get on your nerves and with which you cannot find a relationship. However, it is difficult to discuss esthetic quality for two reasons: first, it is very difficult to communicate visually with words, because the same word can have very different meanings for different people. And secondly, esthetic quality is about nuances, subtle gradations, the harmony and subtle balance of a multitude of visual elements. You need an eye that is trained by years of experience to have a sound judgment here.

4 Good design makes a product understandable

It clarifies the product's structure. Better still, it can make the product talk. At best, it is self-explanatory and saves the frustrating study of incomprehensible operating instructions.

5 Good design is unobtrusive

Products fulfilling a purpose are like tools. They are neither decorative objects nor works of art. Their design should therefore be both neutral and restrained, to leave room for the user's self-expression.

6 Good design is honest

It does not make a product more innovative, powerful or valuable than it really is. It does not attempt to manipulate the consumer with promises that cannot be kept.

7 Good design is long-lasting

It avoids being fashionable and therefore never appears antiquated. Unlike fashionable design, it lasts many years – even in today's throwaway society, for which there is no longer any justification.

8 Good design is thorough down to the last detail

Nothing must be arbitrary or left to chance. Care and accuracy in the design process show respect towards the user.

9 Good design is environmentally-friendly

Design can and must make its contribution to preserving the environment and conserving resources. It must not only do something about physical pollution, but also about visual pollution and destruction of the environment.

10 Good design is as little design as possible

Less, but better – because it concentrates on the essential aspects, and the products are not burdened with non-essentials. Back to purity, back to simplicity.[1]

The thesis that good design is as little as possible design naturally reflects the individual approach of Dieter Rams and has no general validity. Whether products must or can always be unobtrusive and honest leaves a lot of room for interpretation.

Nevertheless, Dieter Rams is regarded as one of the most influential German designers. His consistent approach to design is trendsetting and has influenced many subsequent designers.

If we now attempt to order all the variables that determine a product's design, we can identify four types of factors:

H Human factors (physical, emotional and social user needs)

T Technical factors (material selection and manufacturing process)

E Economic factors (material, tool and labor costs)

E Ecological factors (raw material and energy consumption, environmental impact)

These **product-determining factors** based on Schürer[2] can have different characters from the rational to the irrational with the relevant evaluation criteria ranging accordingly from the objective to subjective. Design has the task of combining all these different, sometimes even contradictory, factors that determine the development of a product into a whole.

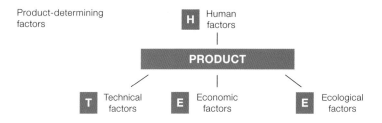

What do we have to do to get from the task to the concrete product? Like every creative process, the design process is also a problem-solving process. To start it off, the problems inherent in the task have to be identified first. This may sound quite simple, but is the first obstacle that has to be overcome. What procedures determine the **problem-solving process** in design?

First of all, there is the **rational-analytic procedure**: it aims at differentiation and breakdown. And then there is the **emotional-intuitive procedure**, which strives for integration and unity. Scientists will stress the rational aspect, while artists will tend towards the intuitive side. When designing consumer goods, both aspects will always interact. After all, human needs (which the products are supposed to meet) also range from the rational to the irrational! Starting out from the "task", you have to work your way up with everything revolving round the "problem" axis. Sometimes you will make progress analytically, then only imaginatively or creatively. Time and again you have to mediate between the two methods – these rungs in the ladder hold the two spirals together, otherwise they would go too far away from the axis and lose sight of the common target.

This design model, which is based on works by F.G. Winter[3] is amazingly similar to the double helix structure of DNA, where the genetic code was discovered as the universal template for all life. Another parallel is to be found in consciousness psychology. The way our brain works can be reduced to two basic functions: in the left half of the brain (which controls the right side of the body) there is cognitive and logical thought, while creativity and intuition are located in the right half (controlling the left side of the body). In our western society we can definitely talk about an overemphasis of the left, rational half of the brain, and perhaps this would explain why many intellectuals are interested in meditation, Zen and other irrational phenomena. Compensation would therefore appear to be emerging here.

Problem solution

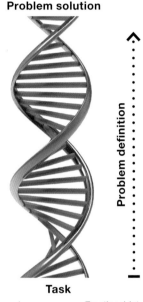

Problem definition

Task

| Rational-analytic procedure | Emotional-intuitive procedure |
| **Knowledge / experience / safety** | **Feeling / imagination / risk** |

Problem-solving process

In our design model, both procedures, the rational-analytic and emotional-intuitive, are joined together logically and help us understand the generally complex design process better.
The next question to be posed in the design process is that of the freedom of form. According to Ingo Klöcker[4] the **freedom of form primarily** depends on the type of product, which will be explained using the following examples. In the case of a drill or turbine vane, the freedom of form is practically zero, as engineering parameters determine the appearance, dimensions and proportions of these products. Design does not make sense here – or the technical function would certainly suffer as a result.

With jewelry or decorative objects, on the other hand, the freedom of form is virtually boundless, as the technical specifications are far less important. Here all kinds of artistic and often also fashionable forms dominate. Between these two extremes lie capital and consumer goods, although the freedom of form is definitely greater in consumer goods. This is due to the usually lesser technical complexity on the one hand, and the users' more individual and therefore more subjective demands on the other.

We can summarize as follows: the freedom of form decreases as the technical complexity increases or use becomes more collective. Conversely, the freedom of form increases as the technical complexity decreases or use becomes more individual.

The **freedom of form** in the area of **capital goods** is usually relatively low. The fully automatic wood shredder shown here combines the tasks of several machines. It produces large quantities of wood chips in a very short time. A great deal of engineering development work is at the core of the product here.
Project work "Schredder der Zukunft" (Shredder of the Future) in cooperation with Komptech.
Design: Christoph Andrejcic and Maximilian Troicher, FH JOANNEUM Industrial Design
Supervisors: Johannes Scherr (Design) and Gerald Steiner (Innovation), FH JOANNEUM Industrial Design

In **fashion design** (jewelry) the **freedom of form** is very high, since the use is very individual.

In **transportation design**, the freedom of form depends on the product language of the respective brand or model series.

Design: Sebastian Vonderau, graduate of FH JOANNEUM Industrial Design

"BMW H2 Concept" is a roadster powered by hydrogen. Master thesis by Philipp Fromme in cooperation with BMW.
Supervisors: Michael Lanz, Lutz Kucher (FH JOANNEUM), Ulrich Ströhle, Hans Steen (BMW), Markus Kremel (BMW Model Making)

The design process – from the idea to volume production

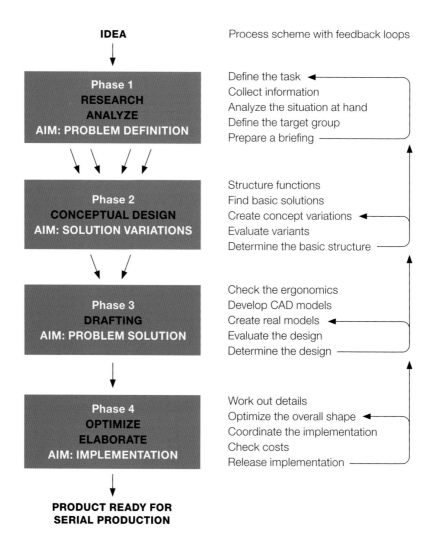

IDEA

Process scheme with feedback loops

Phase 1
RESEARCH
ANALYZE
AIM: PROBLEM DEFINITION

Define the task
Collect information
Analyze the situation at hand
Define the target group
Prepare a briefing

Phase 2
CONCEPTUAL DESIGN
AIM: SOLUTION VARIATIONS

Structure functions
Find basic solutions
Create concept variations
Evaluate variants
Determine the basic structure

Phase 3
DRAFTING
AIM: PROBLEM SOLUTION

Check the ergonomics
Develop CAD models
Create real models
Evaluate the design
Determine the design

Phase 4
OPTIMIZE
ELABORATE
AIM: IMPLEMENTATION

Work out details
Optimize the overall shape
Coordinate the implementation
Check costs
Release implementation

PRODUCT READY FOR
SERIAL PRODUCTION

Let us return to the design process. It can be shown more clearly using a flow chart, although we have to emphasize that it is a schematic model. In practice the process is modified to suit the task in hand and priorities are differently set. It is important to refer to the feedback loops. Whenever feedback shows that a path has not led to the intended goal or an optimum solution, you have to return to the beginning of the loop. This is also necessary if there are new findings while you are working and the situation completely changes as a result (e.g., if a certain material is no longer available, what replacement material could be used and what are the consequences for design?).

Because every design process must be seen within the larger framework of product development it has **interdisciplinary team character**. Experts in various fields, such as marketing, construction, electronics, and manufacturing, work together to solve the problem. Therefore, we will show the relationship between the work phases and the organizational units involved.

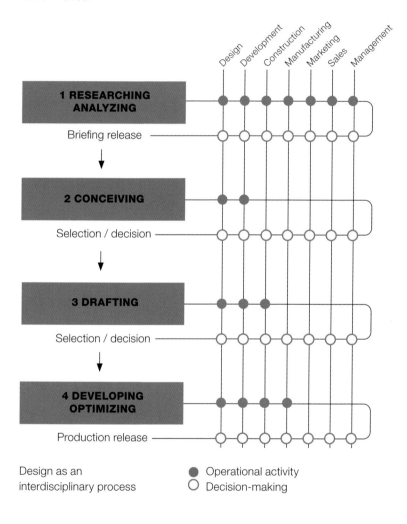

Design as an
interdisciplinary process

● Operational activity
○ Decision-making

List of sources:

(1) Rams, Dieter: Weniger aber besser, Jo Klatt Design+Design Verlag, Hamburg, 1995
(2) Schürer, Arnold: Der Einfluß produktbestimmender Faktoren auf die Gestaltung, Bielefeld, 1974
(3) Winter, Friedrich G.: Gestalten: Didaktik oder Urprinzip, Ravensburg, 1984
(4) Klöcker, Ingo: Produktgestaltung, Berlin, 1981

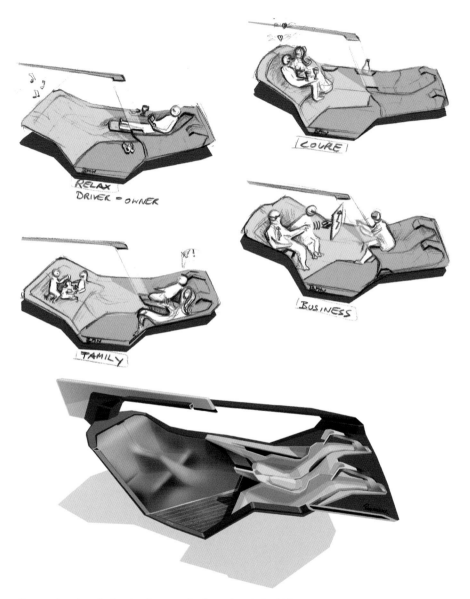

RELAX
DRIVER - OWNER

COUPE

BUSINESS

FAMILY

Research and **analysis** using the example of an automated vehicle:
The technology of the self-propelled car allows us to carry out very different activities when driving in the future. The travel time can be used for meaningful activities such as relaxation, business conferences or board games. Surveys of users and their needs can provide further insights.

Project: "Automated Driving", FH JOANNEUM in cooperation with BMW Group Design Munich
Design and sketches by Daniel Brunsteiner, FH JOANNEUM Industrial Design
Supervisors: Gerhard Friedrich, Christian Bauer, BMW Group Design Munich and Michael Lanz, Marc Ischepp, Miltos Oliver Kounoutras, FH JOANNEUM Industrial Design

Researching and analyzing
Goal: problem identification

The design process starts with setting the task. When defining the task, however, the first mistakes are often made. We should take the following into consideration: an article in daily use always has a useful function. It serves as a problem solver. If, for example, you want to draw a circle on a piece of paper, you can solve the problem by using a pair of compasses, a template or a pin, thread and writing implement. Different solutions and different materials lead to the same goal here. We should not therefore concentrate on the product as the task, but on the problem that is to be solved.

What does this mean for the design process?

We have to get away from "product-oriented" thinking and go for "problem-oriented" work!

Taking lighting as an example: if the task is to develop new lampshades, the scope for ideas is somewhat limited and revolutionary solutions are not to be expected. If, on the other hand, the task is to solve the problem of glare, innovative solutions (e.g., polarizing filters, etc.) are now also conceivable. The task definition therefore has to be oriented towards the users and their needs. It should be worded carefully, but not too narrowly, otherwise there is no chance of arriving at new solution approaches.

Once the task has been defined, the first thing to do is to gather information, i.e., to start the **research**. In practice in design, this means collecting data on the client's and rival products and evaluating it according to various criteria (engineering, ergonomics, market success, etc.). This clearly establishes the advantages and disadvantages of existing products. Furthermore, market analyses are performed, either by evaluating sales statistics or carrying out systematic surveys of representative sections of the population. These procedures are all basically aimed at ascertaining the actual situation and therefore constitute a state analysis.

In addition to market research, target group analysis and need assessment, a product analysis from the consumer's point of view can also be of assistance when performing a state analysis. Comparative analysis of the company's own and rival products can identify the problems inherent in the task, and thus heighten problem awareness, which is so important in the development team.

Such analyses often fail to be carried out due to lack of time or personnel, which is a great disadvantage for problem identification. The same principle applies here as to medicine: it is not the immediately recognizable symptoms of an illness that have to be taken care of, but the deep-seated causes have to be identified and treated accordingly! The former can be compared to superficial window dressing, and the latter to design as a problem-solving process. No medical treatment is possible without thorough diagnosis, and no design process without in-depth analysis.

After starting the process with wide-ranging research into the selected topic (historic development, cultural relationships, technological background, market analyses, etc.), the target group then has to be closely examined. The **target group is defined** – as already mentioned in the "Symbol functions" chapter above – in the form of collages, so-called **mood boards**. Questions are asked: "What do they look like? What do they read? What do they wear? How do they spend their leisure time? What products do they buy?" Catchwords can be derived from the group's world of values, and put together to form a message that the design should subsequently express in its product language (see also page 84).

The findings gleaned from the first stage of research/analysis have to be documented in specifications or data sheets before the second stage can start. They are drawn up in cooperation with all the departments involved in developing a new product (marketing, construction, production, service, etc.). In the case of technically complex products, the specifications or data sheets inevitably end up being huge and unfortunately often confusing documents.

A **design briefing** can be much more effective because it summarizes the factors affecting design in compact form. This tool is of great importance to the entire design process, as it ensures that the results are checked at the end of every stage and the goals set indeed reached.

Presentation of the results from the **research phase** with "Analysis of the Target Group, Trends, Future Mega Trends, Surveys, Products, etc."
Project: "Leica – Die Zukunft der Fotografie" (Leica – The Future of Photography), FH JOANNEUM in cooperation with Leica Camera AG
Supervisors: Michael Lanz, Johannes Scherr, Gerald Steiner, FH JOANNEUM Industrial Design and Mark Shipard, Christoph Gredler, Leica Camera AG

A distinction has to be drawn between two concepts for the briefing:

Demands that must be met, otherwise the solution will not be acceptable (e.g., minimum volume, maximum size, budgeted costs, etc.) and **requests** that should be taken into consideration if possible, but are not absolutely necessary (e.g. stackability, combinability, additional functions, etc.).

A design briefing is generally broken down into the following areas:

Application/target group/market:

Functions, uses
Decisive features
Target group definition
Competition analysis/market situation
Corporate identity

Technical/economic demands:

Technical data (dimensions, weight, etc.)
Environmental conditions (temperature, dampness, etc.)
Operation, maintenance, service life
Process, action
Type of construction, model, assembly, packaging
Requirements, standards, patents, product liability,
quantity, price

Environmental compatibility

Energy and raw material consumption in production and use
Long life, repairable, retrofittable, remountable, recyclable
Reduction in raw materials

Schedule

Development/design/construction
Production planning/market launch

As only a **rough briefing** is often possible in the early stages of product development (which, however, allows greater scope), it can be developed into a **fine briefing** if new findings subsequently come to light.
In practice, small and medium-sized enterprises in particular unfortunately do not spend enough time carefully working out a design briefing and often only hold an oral session!
A good briefing is nevertheless a prerequisite for a successful design process.

Research method/user journey map

Which phases does a glider pilot go through from take-off to landing?

A user journey map visualizes the experiences of interacting with a product or service. Each moment in a sequence of work steps is to be evaluated and improved individually. In the present example, 14 individual steps were analyzed and negative side effects were documented. Through the discussions in the design team, bad user experiences could be revised or made more efficient. User journey maps are usually created next to or following personas and scenarios. Only a thorough research phase can reveal the needs, feelings and perceptions of users. Moreover, negative moments like confusion, stress and frustration should be presented authentically in order to optimize the product or service.

On the ground

1 Equipping
Depending on the aircraft, it can be equipped alone or in pairs.

2 Rolling
Aircraft to be brought into takeoff position. The aircraft must be balanced. (You have to leave the cockpit.)

- Not balanced

3 Getting in
Instruments make boarding more difficult. A high sidewall further enhances the effect.

- Difficult entry

4 Closing the cockpit
The cockpit canopy is closed and locked.

5 Pre-flight check
Instruments are checked and readjusted before departure.

6 The tow rope is hooked in
At the end of the fuselage there is an opening in which the rope is fixed.

- The entire weight is lifted.

Research using the example of a user journey map for a glider.
Project: Master thesis by Alexander Knorr at FH JOANNEUM Industrial Design
Supervisor: Johannes Scherr, FH JOANNEUM Industrial Design (project details see pages 216–227)

7 Acceleration
The airplane must be supported the first few meters, since the speed is still too low and the wing can fall into the grass.

- Not balanced

8 Runway
The glider is still very slow and the pilot has to steer strongly against it to keep the balance.

- Not balanced
- ALARM strikes

9 Departure
The glider is in the air due to the low weight in front of the tow plane. It is flown over the runway at low altitude.

- ALARM strikes

10 Towing
The glider is towed to the release point where it is manually released.

- ALARM strikes

11 Notching
The tow rope is released using the yellow knob. In an emergency, the tow pilot can cut the rope.

12 Flight
The speedometer and the variometer indicate the rate of ascent and descent of the plane.

- Layout is confusing
- ALARM blocks the view

13 Rolling out
On the runway, the plane rolls out until it comes to a standstill and tilts to one side.

- The plane cannot be maneuvered on the ground.

14 Landing approach
The pilot applies the air brakes, which increases the air resistance and the sink rate. This means that the height is quickly lost in a controlled manner.

User journey map in 14 steps from Alexander Knorr's master thesis at FH JOANNEUM Industrial Design
Supervisor: Johannes Scherr, FH JOANNEUM Industrial Design

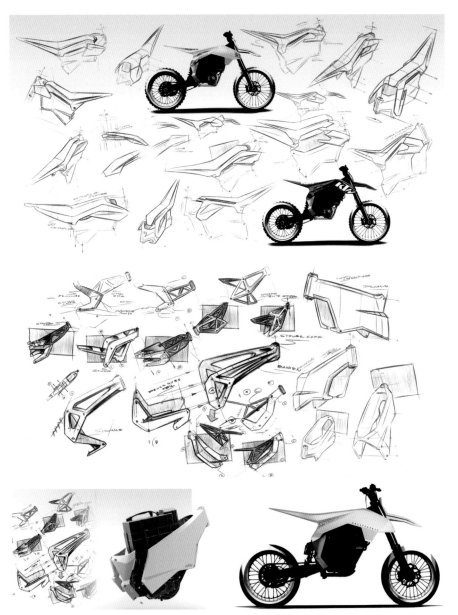

Conceiving using the example of an electric motorcycle:
Under the title "KTM Move Extreme" a new generation of motorcycles was developed, which were equipped with an innovative drive technology (electric motor). The design language of the bike had to be adapted to the new drive technology.

Project: "KTM Move Extreme", FH JOANNEUM Industrial Design in cooperation with KTM and KISKA
Design: Philipp Fromme, FH JOANNEUM Industrial Design
Supervisors: Michael Lanz, Marc Ischepp, Lutz Kucher, FH JOANNEUM and Christoph Täubl, KISKA

Conceiving

Goal: alternative solutions

In the concept phase, product language, use-oriented and technical **basic solutions** are developed in parallel first, which are then logically combined. What is decisive when drawing up these concepts is as **wide a range as possible of options or alternative solutions**. Do not therefore apply the brakes too early just because "we've never done it like that before", but allow the unconventional or unusual. Only then can innovative solutions be found – restrictions will come soon enough!

As far as the procedure in the concept phase is concerned, there is commonly a fundamental difference between the constructor and the designer. Given that the overall function is usually divided into individual areas, the constructor is used to searching for individual solutions first and then putting them together to form an overall concept. The designer, on the other hand, is more like a sculptor as a rule, going from "the rough to the fine", i.e., from a comprehensive – sometimes visionary – overall concept to a detailed solution. This can sometimes meet with a lack of understanding because the intuitive generalist clashes with the rational pragmatist. But we need both characters for product development, and should do everything in our power to prevent a collision course.

In many cases, however, the overall function required by the task also has to be structured by the designer, i.e., divided up rationally into primary and secondary functions. Only then is the task, which consists of a whole collection of connected problems, manageable and can be tackled step by step. Now, how can a problem be structured? We will describe a method that comes from value analysis.

The function structure

The starting point for our considerations is an existing product. It is seen as an active system, which consists of various parts, the elements. The active system fulfils the overall function, while the various elements are vehicles for the individual functions.

Functions are always described using a noun and a verb (an active one if possible), e.g., turn a wheel, draw a hexagon or split a stone.

To arrive at a function description, we have to ask: "What does the product do as a whole?" (= overall function) and "What does the specific element do?" (= individual function).

We will illustrate this process by taking a **flashlight**[1] as an example. First of all, we have to describe the product and its elements quite clearly in order to derive the product and element functions. It is still about the product-related actual situation, but shown in a structured function chart. To enable new solutions to the problem to be found, however, we have to depart from the actual situation and abstract further: the product function becomes the overall function, and the element function the individual one.

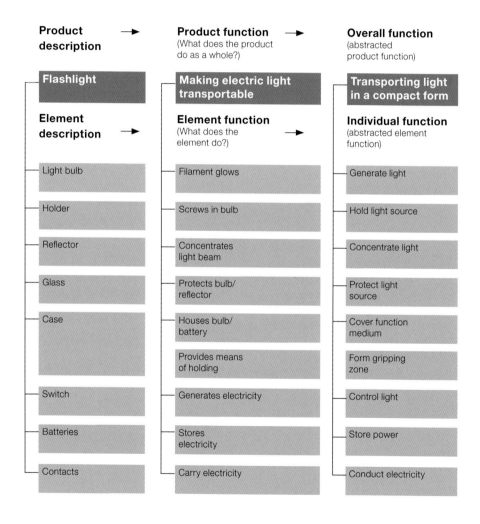

Product description →	Product function → (What does the product do as a whole?)	Overall function (abstracted product function)
Flashlight	**Making electric light transportable**	**Transporting light in a compact form**
Element description →	Element function → (What does the element do?)	Individual function (abstracted element function)
Light bulb	Filament glows	Generate light
Holder	Screws in bulb	Hold light source
Reflector	Concentrates light beam	Concentrate light
Glass	Protects bulb/ reflector	Protect light source
Case	Houses bulb/ battery	Cover function medium
	Provides means of holding	Form gripping zone
Switch	Generates electricity	Control light
Batteries	Stores electricity	Store power
Contacts	Carry electricity	Conduct electricity

This departure from product-oriented to function and therefore problem-oriented thinking is extremely important to the design process, as it broadens the horizon when searching for ideas.

In our example, the ultimate abstraction of functions not only describes a flashlight, but also a Stone Age torch and a fluorescent light for divers based on advanced photochemical technology. To remain with the flashlight example: having divided up its functions, the problem has also been broken down and the overall problem separated into individual areas. We can therefore move on to the next step.

To stick to the flashlight example: after structuring the problem and breaking it down into partial problems, the next partial steps can ne tackled.

Several solution principles have to be found for every individual function:

e.g. storing power:
- batteries (round/flat)
- rechargeable batteries (charge by plugging into mains, use solar cells, etc.)

e.g. generating light:
- bulb
- halogen lamp
- light-emitting diades (LEDs)

After having found solution principles for every individual function, you can put these individual solutions together to produce initial alternative concepts, taking the briefing into consideration. These concepts follow the guidelines for the theoretical structure of the problem solution. In our example two alternative concepts could look like this:

Concept A: flashlight with a flat case.
Three to four low consumption LEDs arranged in a row and protected by the protruding case collar. Rechargeable batteries charged by solar cells on the top of the case. Switch on by lightly squeezing the two case halves together.

Concept B: flashlight with a round case.
One halogen lamp, compact shape similar to a pen, linear batteries, reflector integrated in the case and protected by a transparent cover. Switch on by turning the two case cylinders in opposite directions.

Either concept A or B will be chosen on the basis of the briefing.

Freehand sketches (line drawings) from the concept phase

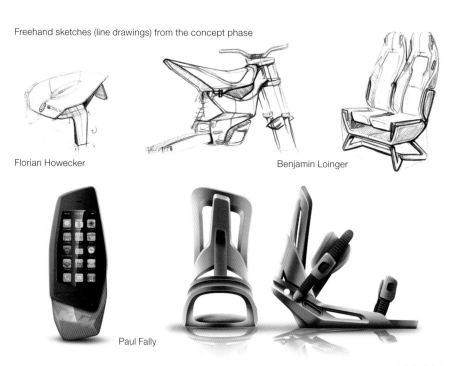

Florian Howecker

Benjamin Loinger

Paul Fally

Michal Holzer

Stefan Märzendorfer

Alexander Knorr

Photoshop renderings (rendering sketches) created on Wacom's interactive graphics tablet.
Presentation techniques of the lecture "Digital Design Tools", Johannes Scherr, FH JOANNEUM

Regarding the **methods of representation** in the concept phase:

In product design the designers will usually show their different concepts in the form of **freehand sketches** (line drawings and/or renderings) and **working models** (proportional or structural models). An important working basis is the **package drawing**, which shows all the important modules schematically in the right arrangement.

The **proportional model** – also called working, preliminary or dimension model – is usually made of materials that are easy to work with (e.g., foam, cardboard or wood), as constant alterations, improvements and modifications tend to be the rule.
Modeling can be described as three-dimensional design and is very important because the proportions of a three-dimensional object, for example, cannot be judged as a whole until the model has been built.

A **structural model,** on the other hand, shows the load-bearing, constructively effective structure as proof of strength, safety or feasibility. In the models the optimum scale is real size, i.e., 1:1. Not only the real visual effect, but also haptic and ergonomic qualities can then be checked more efficiently, such as handle shapes, etc. The requirements for an **ergonomic model** may also be met at the same time. Typical examples: hairdryer, telephone, drill. In the case of larger objects, smaller scales have to be selected as appropriate.

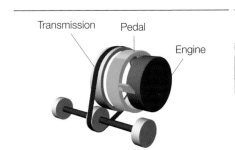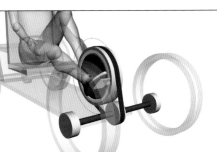

Package representations of a pedal drive with supporting electric motor. Design: Isabella Zidek, Joscha Herold, FH JOANNEUM Industrial Design (details on the project see pages 178–193)

Working models within the framework of the Dyson Workshop at FH JOANNEUM Industrial Design

Proportion model of a handsaw, design: Tim Hinderhofer, FH JOANNEUM Industrial Design

In **transportation design**, freehand drawings are called **sketches** and we therefore talk about the sketch phase. The demands placed on the quality and variety of these renderings are very high and sketching is therefore often a separate course in the study of design.

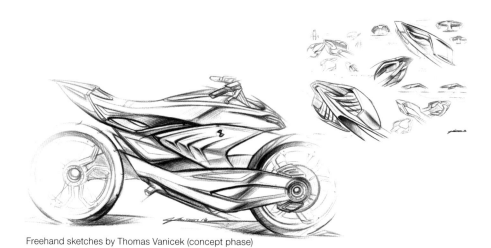

Freehand sketches by Thomas Vanicek (concept phase)

Photoshop rendering by Thomas Vanicek (concept phase)

Photoshop rendering of the BMW e1 electric bike (concept phase). Master thesis by Thomas Vanicek at FH JOANNEUM Industrial Design in cooperation with BMW Motorrad.

One last remark about the **range of different concepts and alternatives:** ideally the solutions would range from a pragmatic-classic approach to the innovative-progressive and visionary-futuristic. This gives the company great freedom of choice.

The risk it is willing to take chiefly depends on its strategic position, the market situation and target group behavior.

American star designer Raymond Loewy recommends following his MAYA principle in this respect[2]:

 **Most Advanced, Yet Acceptable!**

As progressive as possible, but not to the extent of being rejected by the customer!

Clients make a selection from several different concepts with the help of the specifications or data sheets and in consultation with all the departments involved in the product development. Having carefully weighed up all the arguments, as a rule they will release one and in exceptional cases two design concepts for further improvement.

List of sources:

(1) Heufler, Gerhard: Produkt-Design, ...von der Idee zur Serienreife, Linz, 1987
(2) Loewy, Raymond: Hässlichkeit verkauft sich schlecht, Düsseldorf, 1992

Drafting using the example of a portable lamp:
The portable lamp Umbra has a clear function that is oriented to the needs of the user. Its flexibility in the various application areas makes the lamp an innovative and unique product for an urban environment. The lamp can be used in the children's room (with direct or indirect light), at outdoor events or as a pendant lamp in the living room. The development of a product family enables the company to enter the consumer sector and thus gain access to a new group of buyers.

Project: Master thesis at FH JOANNEUM in cooperation with XAL
Design: Florian Blamberger, supervisor: Johannes Scherr, FH JOANNEUM Industrial Design

Drafting

Goal: problem solution

We have now reached the core of the design process, the draft stage. In the analytic phase it was mainly a case of logical thinking, whereas in the concept phase rational thinking is now combined with intuitive, creative approaches. In the draft stage the focus is even more on the creative area, as it is now a case of implementing the often only very rough concept with the theoretical product structure in accurate, practically oriented – and therefore economically viable – drafts.

This implementation stage in particular presents a variety of problems. What may have looked very good in the conceptional sketch often proves not to be feasible when worked at more thoroughly. How do you solve such problems?

There are three possible ways:

1. Trial and error
2. Waiting for inspiration
3. Methodical problem solution

The first two options are well known and can look back on a long tradition. They also have the disadvantage, however, of usually taking a lot of time and not always meeting with success. In industry people have therefore been puzzling for some time as to how the success rate in problem solving could be increased and the time involved decreased. The result is a large number of methods for systematically generating ideas, which are usually carried out in groups and have primarily bee developed for complex tasks.

Three simple methods are described in brief below.

1 Classic brainstorming

Description: Special form of intensive group discussion without time for reflection aimed at producing creative ideas. The following rules should be observed: every participant is entitled to develop and voice thoughts without inhibition. Each one should pick up ideas put forward in the group as suggestions and explore them further. Criticism is not permissible during the discussion. Killer phrases (e.g., that won't work, that costs too much, we've already had that before, etc.) are banned.
Quantity takes priority over quality. Reason and logic are not initially of great importance. To ensure that no ideas get lost, all the suggestions made during the discussion should immediately be written on the blackboard visible to everyone or, better still, on a poster or brown paper (so that they can also serve as a reminder later).

2 Destructive-constructive brainstorming

Description: In the first phase all the weaknesses of a problem, (e.g., in a product development, are collected in a brainstorming session. In the second phase solutions are then sought for all the weaknesses also using brainstorming. This raises problem awareness within a very short space of time, and the first suggestions for solutions can be made. Particularly suitable for redesign tasks.

3 Analogy

This is a method that is used very successfully in research and development. It demands spontaneity, imagination and a talent for improvisation. Just how successfully it is already used in practice becomes clear if you think of the freely suspended cable net roof for Munich's Olympic stadium: the analogy with a spider's web is immediately apparent. That would be one example of bionics[1] where potential solutions to technical problems are sought in nature. These are examined to determine their function principle and then applied to the relevant problem. A typical example from the field of bionics:

Problem: a mobile radio antenna with the following properties is to be developed:
- 20 meters high
- very light (to be carried by one person)
- to be put up and taken down in a very short time
- and small when collapsed

Block: the experts cannot get away from the telescope principle. Creativity is inhibited.
The solution is to make the question more general and draw analogies: what in nature is long and thin, but also very agile?
A snake, chameleon's tongue, giraffe's neck, monkey's tail...
They opted for the giraffe's neck.

Analysis: a visit to the natural history museum enlightened our experts as to the function principle: vertebrae located one above the other are held together and moved with muscles and tendons.
Transfer and solution: plastic cylindrical parts with a center bore and a flexible steel lead (the actual antenna) running through it. If the lead is taut, the vertebrae are straightened and stabilized. When the tension is released, the antenna can be moved and easily rolled up.

This example is also ideal for showing what is generally important when solving problems. Namely:

Solving a problem means: | **departing completely from the problem!**

First the concrete problem has to be generalized to enable new analogies to be sought in completely different areas ("departing from the problem"). Once you have discovered potential solutions, you return to the original problem and examine them to see if they are suitable for an innovative approach.

Since the preparation for tackling the problem involves a lot of analytic work, it is not that easy to be calm and creative. As a result, the first spontaneous solutions are usually relatively conventional. It is, however, good, or even necessary, to rid yourself of such spontaneous solutions (which everyone has at the ready) by presenting them to the group. As in brainstorming, they must not be "killed" or further development may be blocked with frustration. Ridding yourself of the first ideas makes you free for the work to come. Now it is a case of departing from the problem. Which is why you have to be detached to find analogies in a completely different field, e.g., nature in the case of a technical problem. Let your imagination run riot. The same applies here: no "killer" phrases! Take advantage of every idea and discuss it.

Only by getting rid of the first ideas one becomes free for further work. Now we have to get rid of the problem: therefore, the outbreak in analogies into a far away area, e.g., to get help from nature in case of a technical problem. Now the imagination can fully come into play.

Also here applies: no "killer phrases"! All ideas should be taken up and discussed.

Finding ideas by drawing analogies confirms that it is not specialized knowledge, but as comprehensive an all-round education as possible, coupled with imagination and unconventional thinking that leads to success. Specialized knowledge again plays an important role when implementing the ideas.

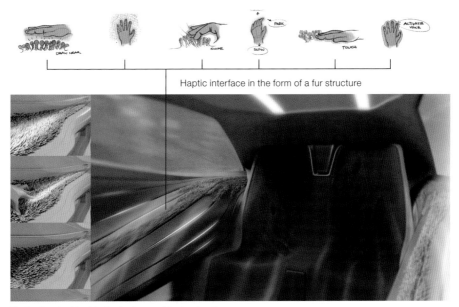

Haptic interface in the form of a fur structure

Design inspired by bionics (nature and technology):
The project work "BMW I am" deals with the symbiosis between man and machine. The interaction with the vehicle takes place via an intuitive haptic interface, a kind of fur structure just below the glass pane. This emphasizes the liveliness of the machine. It strengthens the growing relationship between user and machine over time and thus creates the necessary trust and acceptance of fully autonomous locomotion.

Project: "Automated Driving", FH JOANNEUM in cooperation with BMW Group Design Munich
Design: Jan Ernhardt, Jenny Gebler, Laura Lang, Marian Massegg, FH JOANNEUM Industrial Design
Supervisors: Gerhard Friedrich, Christian Bauer, BMW Group Design Munich (Design) and
Michael Lanz, Marc Ischepp and Oliver Kountouras, FH JOANNEUM Industrial Design

The antenna example also makes the way **creativity** works clearer. In simplified terms, it is combining familiar elements, principles or functions in a completely new way. The principle of the radio antenna was just as well known as the giraffe's neck. But nobody had ever combined the two in this way before!

Being creative therefore means thinking laterally,
i.e., going for breadth and remaining open minded.

We can learn something else from the example: the more varied a person's experience, skills and knowledge, the better the chances for innovative, unconventional solutions. Even the best designers can reach their limits when faced with some problems. If it is a question of highly specialized requirements, for example, controlling or operating complex devices, a specialist may be called in to help the designer. In this case it could be an ergonomics expert or occupational physician.

At the end of this draft phase, an evaluation on the basis of a briefing or the specifications is again required. Other experts may possibly be consulted to help the in-house team check that all the requirements have been met. If there is a choice of options, they will now have to agree on one suggestion. Should none of the options meet the specifications, they will first have to check whether the specifications contain requirements that are impossible to meet under the given circumstances and have to be amended as a result. If the problem lies with the draft, however, a new approach has to be taken and a loop back to the concept phase may also be necessary.

Only in very few cases does the design process have a purely linear structure. The chaos theory has provided us with some scientifically backed explanations, which used to be simply but aptly described as "creative chaos".

Methods of representation:

Worthy of mention here are also the **methods of representation** that are generally used in the draft phase. While freehand sketches (line drawings or rendering sketches) are most common in the concept phase, in this phase it is **schematic sections, explosion drawings** and **perspective views** in addition to scale projections. Nowadays 3-D CAD software is primarily used for these tasks.

Explosion diagrams of a household appliance for the quick and easy production of tofu using hot air. Preparation at home guarantees the desired freshness.

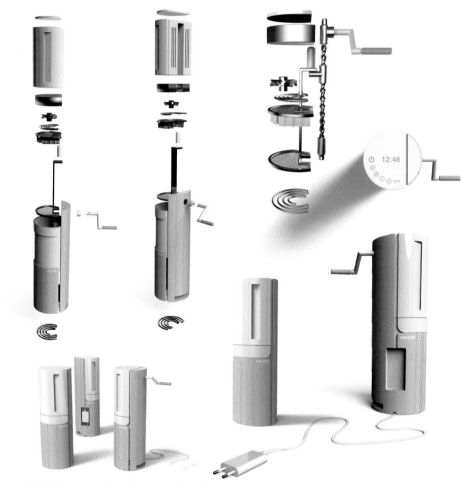

3-D CAD representation of a household appliance

Project: "Cooking with Air", FH JOANNEUM in cooperation with Philips Austria GmbH
Design: Elisabeth Schmeißl, FH JOANNEUM Industrial Design
Supervisors: Johannes Scherr (Design) and Matthias Götz (Ergonomics), FH JOANNEUM Industrial Design

Virtual models can be rendered photorealistically. This is done with the help of ray tracing, which enables complex shadows, reflections and refracted light to be calculated. These virtual models can be inserted in a suitable environment or animated, often dispensing with the need for time-consuming modeling.

Photorealistic virtual model in transportation design:
The automotive industry offers the possibility to assemble products according to their own needs with the help of color and material selection. This is referred to as "personalizing products". The exterior and interior are adapted to the customer's wishes on site using predefined elements. Virtual models provide realistic images with the help of appropriate software.

Project: Master thesis at FH JOANNEUM Industrial Design in cooperation with Smart
Design: Michael Pacher (Supervisor: Georg Wagner, FH JOANNEUM)

A few remarks about this subject from practical experience: CAD plays a relatively minor role in the concept phase, as sketching by hand is much faster. In addition, CAD always requires precise data. This may be taken for granted by the constructor, but the designer works more like a sculptor from the "roug" to the "fine". Computers are therefore constantly gaining in importance after the concept phase, and the optimizing and implementing phases are virtually inconceivable without them now (rapid prototyping).

CAD is an extremely valuable tool, which makes various different options and simulation much easier with virtual models and therefore often leads to faster customer decisions. What the computer still cannot replace is sensitivity and creativity.

In addition to the two-dimensional representation methods, models are now also frequently used in the draft phase. They may be proportional or design models, or else function and ergonomic models. Full-scale models are always the best, but in the case of larger products the time and costs involved mean they are no longer feasible. Here a smaller scale model or high-quality computer renderings may be acceptable solutions. The design model (often also called mock-up) may look like the finished product, but does not work as yet. An advantage of the design model is that photos can be taken for the first customer brochures. A function model, on the other hand, checks that the technical details function properly (e.g., clip-on device) irrespective of the design. Similarly, an ergonomic model may test the operation of controls or the haptic quality of a handle.

Virtual models deliver photorealistic images with the help of appropriate software. The environment can be supplemented by image montage and reflections on reflective surfaces can be calculated.

List of sources:

(1) Nachtigall, Werner/Blüchel, Kurt G.: Das große Buch der Bionik, Munich, 2003

Developing and optimizing

Goal: implementation

In this phase the draft continues to be examined and optimized in relation to construction, manufacturing technologies and materials. Therefore, the designer also needs basic skills in these fields – only then can successful solutions be found together with the experts.

While the previous phase was a considerable challenge in terms of creativity, the work in the final phase is again more logical and rational. It is a question of working out the details together with the constructors, i.e., optimizing the overall draft, not only regarding design, but also technical and financial aspects. All the components have to be checked again with respect to construction, material selection and manufacturing technology to allow process planning.

To maximize cost effectiveness, other methods, such as **value analysis**, are also advisable. This systematic examination is a common means of cutting costs in Japanese companies, but still seldom used in other countries. Design is therefore transferred from development construction to production construction, which requires intensive dialog between the engineer and designer.

The methods of representation are essentially as described above, but also include some other modeling techniques. Given the changes or optimization that proves necessary, the design model, also called mock-up or presentation model, is not built until the final form exists. It has to be produced to the highest modeling standards, as it has to represent the exterior perfectly and allow the first photos to be taken for brochures. The work involved is very complex and requires appropriate qualifications. Professional modelers therefore do the work in most cases.

After the specifications have been checked, the preparation phase is completed and approval given to draw up the production documents. These documents, which include **exact workshop drawings**, detail drawings and assembly drawings – all generated using CAD – are produced by the development constructors and in turn also have to be checked by the designer.

Often only slight changes have to be made, but they can affect the design significantly, and are therefore not to be underestimated.

At this point in time the product has been defined down to the last detail, with the result that nothing now stands in the way of building one or more prototypes. Prototypes are fully functional and virtually correspond to the vehicle subsequently, to be manufactured, except that only one is made at a time.

Rapid prototyping is a means of producing a full-sized model using various technologies. Stereolithography is the most widely used prototyping technology, perfectly combining CAD and CAM. It builds plastic models of even the most complex shaped objects within a short space of time by tracing a laser beam on a vat of liquid photopolymer.

During the subsequent **prototype testing**, all the functions are thoroughly checked and result in further optimization of the production documents and reviewing of the estimated costs.
The time has then come for the management to make the final decision regarding production release. As a rule this means making the tools required – not only a time-consuming, but also a cast-intensive process.

The next step is checking the first **pilot lot sample** that is produced with the new tools. Here the very last faults should be detected and corrected before the product is released for volume production.

The description of this phase clearly shows that it not only makes sense for the designer to be involved in the development process right up to the pilot lot, but is also absolutely necessary. Otherwise there would be a risk of the painstakingly produced design becoming unbalanced in the final hectic throes of the work, if not ruined.

When preparing for production, the documentation, user manuals, brochures and PR material – everything required for market launch and sales – also has to be organized and produced. The design has now reached the **production stage**.

Optimization and elaboration using the example of a hybrid equipment carrier. Different attachments can be docked to a basic module, mainly for agricultural use. The functions of the attachments range from mowers and snow blowers to fire-fighting modules.

The first generation of the equipment carrier shown on the left has been further developed in a comprehensive design process in terms of design and technology. Above we see the design draft as 3-D visualization and below the design presentation model, which was created with a large number of 3-D-printed parts on the basis of a high-quality CAD model.

Inspired by a "naked bike", at the end of the design process three deep-drawn moulded parts were developed, which are connected by a spatial tubular frame. All other machine components such as batteries, controls, etc. were accommodated in standardized black boxes and not covered.

The design goal was to achieve maximum product identity and functionality with as few attachments as possible. The lateral cladding parts form the visual center of the working machine and give the HYMOG its unmistakable appearance.

Project: PTH HYMOG
Client: PTH Products Maschinenbau, Neuberg/Austria
Design: Johannes Scherr by Johannes Scherr Design

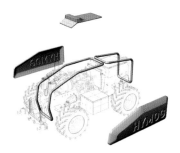 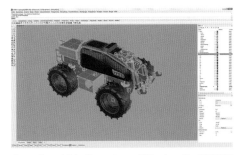

In CAD, the stainless steel frame was stretched over the entire vehicle like a clamp. This gives the HYMOG high quality and robustness. On the roof there is a powerful LED headlight.

The prototype of the new equipment carrier has been extensively tested in various application scenarios such as snow clearance or fire fighting. Only after the successful interplay of all attachments was series production approved.

An important field of application for the HYMOG is landscape maintenance. The wheels are driven electrically and the attachments are powered by a combustion engine. The control can be carried out via a radio remote control or as an autonomous unit (similar to a mowing robot).

Factors in a successful design process

To round off the chapter on "Design as a process", we would like to report on what experience freelance designers and independent design studios have had with companies. What recommendations can we draw from them?

The size of the company

Nowadays it goes without saying that there are in-house design departments in larger companies, but in small and medium-sized enterprises they are only worthwhile in exceptional cases, such as highly design-oriented fields. But even firms with their own design departments frequently bring in freelance designers for development work, on the one hand to increase the range of solutions suggested and on the other to counteract potential blindness to the company's shortcomings.

Small and medium-sized enterprises very often argue that they are simply too small to work with a designer. An example: a cursory glance at an industrially oriented sector shows that all the energy goes into engineering, but the innovation produced is usually only "packaged" conventionally and unimaginatively. Therefore, the enormous effort that went into development cannot be seen from the product design, the innovation undersells itself – and an advantage is thoughtlessly thrown away. Even a small company can no longer afford to do so in view of today's competitive situation. There can be no lower limit for company size.

The experience gained in this field can be summarized as follows: small and medium-sized enterprises are usually better at cooperating efficiently with freelance designers because they tend to be more easily manageable, flexible and have clearer decision-making powers than many a large corporate group.

The type of company

If you divide up manufacturers into the consumer and capital goods sectors, you will find that the former group tends to have been cooperating with designers for some time.

In the capital goods sector, on the other hand, consulting designers still does not go without saying. Many companies think that cutting edge technology is enough to be competitive. In addition, why should you design a module, for example, that you won't see later – as it is installed out of sight? But here in particular design has the task of making the inner qualities visible outwardly. At presentations for trade fairs or the customer, the product language is often decisive because it conveys quality.

The selection of the designer

Here the company should carefully examine several questions: does the designer's profile fit the task? Does he already have experience in the relevant product sector or with the target group addressed? Or could a "fresh" designer in this special field give new impetus and come up with better ideas?

Will the task permit trouble-free cooperation at a distance? Telephone, fax and e-mail facilitate communication, but cannot completely replace face-to-face discussion. Or would it be better for the designer to be based locally so that he could be available in person at any time, e.g., for complex optimization or corrective steps?

Whether preference should be given to a larger or smaller design office depends on the task, the kind of cooperation, and also whether you are on the same wavelength. The more complex the task, the more important the ability becomes to cooperate constructively with the various departments. Only if the team is capable of creating a working atmosphere based on mutual trust can optimum results be expected. Affected or pretentious behavior is totally out of place.

In the case of particularly problematic tasks, a competition may be the answer. Several designers are invited independently to present a design study – with an exact briefing, clearly defined scope and the same fee. This broadens the range of solutions suggested, but means more time and effort. The winner of the competition is then generally asked to take charge of the project.

One last tip for choosing the designer: if a company has never worked with a designer before, it should select one with considerable practical experience. This minimizes the risk of a failed design process. A company with experience of designers, on the other hand, can definitely be given food for thought by a designer as yet unburdened by practical experience and can thus get out of a rut.

The beginning of cooperation

This is where the first mistake is often made: the designer is involved in the development process far too late when engineering decisions have already determined the form. Design is now either reduced to window dressing or leads to radical technical changes, which in turn result in delays, added expenses and also frustration among the engineers. Early involvement in the process is a must if the contribution of design is to be coordinated efficiently with the relevant development steps. Ideally, technical concepts and design concepts should stimulate and inspire each other.

The second mistake often made at the start of cooperation is no briefing or only an inadequate one (or specifications, data sheet or list of requirements). A successful design process can only be built on solid foundations: a briefing that has involved all the departments working on the development. The task should not be defined too narrowly on the one hand, otherwise new ideas may be excluded from the outset, and on the other, it should be precise enough not to build castles in the air. It may also make sense to begin with rough specifications first and then add the finer points later. The more comprehensively and intensely a task and the problems involved are discussed and analyzed, the more focused the entire development process will be. Overriding corporate goals play just as much a role here as product-oriented marketing strategies, target group issues and manufacturing problems – the designer therefore has to be involved right from the beginning.

The design services

When selecting a designer, you are faced with the task of weighing up various offers. The assignment will revolve around product design in most cases, but the services provided by larger offices may range from market research to prototyping. Once the decision has been taken, the design services have to be carefully coordinated in relation to the development process and in-house facilities. Is it only a question of reworking an existing product, i.e., redesign, or a completely new development?
Are the relevant ergonomic studies, constructive concepts or corporate design required?
Could a design study with subsequent optimization phase be enough or does it have to be broken down into individual development steps?
The services also have to be clarified regarding modeling: are proportional, functional or design models required? Are they part of the design work, will they be outsourced or some made in-house?
An exact description of the services required tailored to the relevant task should therefore be included in the quotation.

The design fee

A distinction is usually drawn between payment by performance and by results. The former includes the flat rate (particularly suitable for primarily creative services, such as design studies) and billing on the basis of hourly or daily rates (which are mainly used for optimization phases where the scope is difficult to estimate).
Payment by results normally means a per-unit fee on the basis of the ex works price. Sometimes a combination of the above fees is used with a flat rate and, for example, a per-unit fee. The rule of thumb here is the higher the design's share is considered to be in the product turnover, the more likely payment will be based on a success-related fee (e.g., in all highly esthetically oriented areas). The greater the share of engineering in the development work, the more seldom a success-related fee is charged (e.g., in the capital goods sector).

The combination of payment by performance and by results has, however, proved itself in practice because it ensures high motivation and continuity in subsequent project support. Not to be forgotten is an agreement on the costs incurred in addition to the fees, such as travel expenses, modeling costs, photo fees, etc.

The occasional practice of providing the design services first and making the payment of the fee dependent on whether the customer is satisfied or not is dubious and neither offered nor accepted by professional designers.

As far as the design costs are concerned, it can be said that they are generally relatively low in relation to the total development costs, but are constantly gaining in significance as a factor in quality and therefore competition. In successful product development, design is a cost factor that has to be budgeted for just like, say, marketing or construction.

In addition to the necessary hardware components (PC, laptop, tablet for drawing, etc.), an industrial design workstation also includes a large number of software packages that must be taken into account in the hourly fee.

The basic conditions

What other factors have to be taken into consideration to ensure that the product design process runs smoothly?
Here are a few tips gained from practical experience:
Design is a matter for top-level management! It is not window dressing at a later date, but a strategic tool.

Teamspirit

The development team must be comprehensive. This means that the experts in all the areas involved must take part in all the decisive design meetings. As a rule these fields are marketing, development, production and management. The staff costs may sometimes appear to be relatively high when a large number of expensive employees get together frequently, but it is worth it! Firstly, high identification with the project is ensured right from the beginning and secondly, only then can efficient coordination of all the development steps be achieved. If, for example, the employee responsible for service was not involved in the task or briefing, and does not encounter the new development until the final phase, he will be frustrated on discovering that the service problems have not been solved optimally. Consequently, often expensive changes could have been avoided and the working atmosphere would not have suffered if this department had also been integrated in the development process in good time.

Innovative solutions in a team

When starting to work with a company, freelance designers will feel like outsiders to a certain extent because they naturally cannot have all the background information desirable. It is therefore very important for mutual trust to be built up and the team to pursue the same goals.

Designers have to draw on the experience and knowhow of the specialists involved in the product development if they are to produce sound creative work. An arrogant, know-all attitude on the part of the designer would be just as out of place here as blocking by the experts. We must not forget that the designer is a generalist in interdisciplinary terms, and therefore has to be supplied with all the project-related information by the company. Only then is there a guarantee that all the product-determining factors in product design will be networked. (The designer naturally undertakes not to divulge any trade secrets). Conversely, the designer ought to be given the requisite freedom as a specialist in creativity. Only if there is enough creative space can innovative solutions be found.

What is important for problem-free communication between the designer and the interdisciplinary development team is a competent contact. In most cases it will be the project or research and development manager. His task is primarily to be seen in design management, including all the coordination and information work concerned. Decisive for efficient design management is, of course, the involvement in corporate management.

Design should not be an ad hoc measure, but an ongoing and integral part of corporate strategy!

User-centric solutions through participative design

If you want to develop user-centric solutions, you first have to understand the users. What needs do they have, what painpoints do existing solutions have? This information can be determined through user insights. Participative design goes one step further by turning stakeholders into participants in the product development process in order to make their ideas usable for product improvement. The aim of this participatory design process is to test existing hypotheses for optimizing the design and the user processes and to develop new hypotheses together with the users and to jointly test their meaningfulness. One method of participative design is a co-creation workshop, which is conducted with the participation of users, designers, usability experts and design researchers. By simulating different usage situations, existing problems are identified and at the same time new solution approaches are developed jointly by the participants, which can then be evaluated in the workshop with the aid of simple prototypes. It is important that this workshop is professionally moderated and takes place in a special set-up.

A part of this set-up is that the usage situation is simulated with simplified props in order to create a film or stage-like atmosphere. This helps the users to approach the solution of problems in a more playful way and to express not completely well thought-out solutions through the improvised situation.

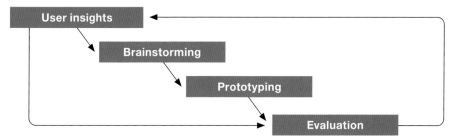

Diagram of the course of a one-day workshop. The phases shown can be repeated several times a day.

A good example of a successful co-creation process is the development of the Siemens SOMATOM go.Up CT platform. Here, designers, researchers and usability specialists from designaffairs and Siemens spent several months developing new hardware and software as well as an intelligent operating concept for the computer tomography platform. An essential part of this process was to conduct several co-creation workshops in different countries with the participation of medical-technical radiology assistants (MTRA), who work with such systems on a daily basis. Through the participation of the users, the operating procedures and the workflow of the entire system could be significantly improved by optimizing the hardware and software.

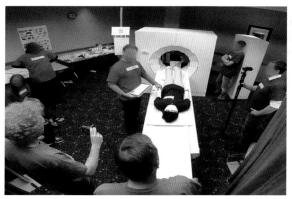

Siemens SOMATOM go. co-creation workshop: workshop situation with mockups, participants and moderators in Dallas, USA

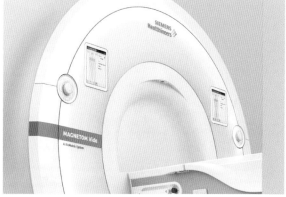

The Siemens MAGNETOM Vida MTR scanner with an image of the tablet-based control element

The design process in transportation design

Transportation design has established a specific design process, which is explained on the following pages. The presented project work from the master's degree was developed in cooperation with BMW Group Design Munich and is dedicated to the topic of automated driving. This chapter shows the development of a design study including a presentation model. The design methods used and the model building techniques require specific tools and machines. Many sketches were made, so-called tape renderings were created with the help of tapes, digitally drawn on the interactive drawing board and a clay model built. During the subsequent digitization of the clay model, a 3-D scanner and special software were used. From the revised virtual 3-D model, a true-to-scale design model was then created using a CNC milling machine and 3-D printer technology. The following overview shows the individual work steps and the working methods used.

RESEARCH / CONCEPT	**Developing the first rough proportions and functions of the vehicle** Methods: package presentations, seat boxes, concept sketches, brainstorming, workshop, etc.
↓	
DRAFT	**Form finding using hand sketches, renderings, tape renderings and clay models** Methods: sketches, tape renderings, clay modeling, renderings, etc.
↓	
REVERSE ENGINEERING	**The path from the real clay model to the virtual model using a 3-D scan** Method: scanning the clay model, editing the scanner data and creating a new CAD model for the interior and exterior
↓	
IMPLEMENTATION	**From virtual CAD model to real presentation model** Method: finally, a true-to-scale model is produced mechanically using a CNC milling machine or 3-D printer and the individual parts of the model are finished by hand using precision work (grinding, priming and painting)

Virtual CAD model

Real presentation model

BMW xBase – Automated Driving 2030

Project work at FH JOANNEUM in cooperation with BMW Group Design.
Exterior design: Benjamin Loinger, Jean-Marc Wilkens, FH JOANNEUM
Interior design: Clara Feßler, Luis Meixner, FH JOANNEUM
Supervisors: Gerhard Friedrich and Christian Bauer, BMW Group Design
Michael Lanz, Marc Ischepp and Miltos Oliver Kountouras, FH JOANNEUM Industrial Design
Walter Lach, Petrus Gartler, Miltos Oliver Kountouras (model making), FH JOANNEUM

Subject
Automated driving is an important topic for BMW, as it is for other car manufacturers. Independent control of vehicles will massively change the design of the interior, as the demands and free spaces of passengers will change dramatically. The following question was therefore important for BMW: How can BMW's brand values be brought to life in the exterior and interior of an automatically driving vehicle?

Vehicle concept
The BMW xBASE is the ideal companion for sports activities. Designed for a wide variety of sports, such as mountain biking, climbing or surfing, the vehicle supports the user in planning, takes him to the ideal starting point, offers recreational opportunities during breaks and picks him up again at the end of the tour. The functional outer surface facilitates the transport of a wide range of sports equipment. This makes the compact BMW xBASE ideal for urban use.

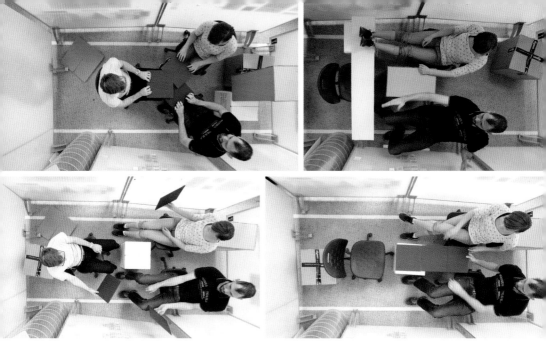

Package

The package drawing is a common type of representation in transportation design. The most important assemblies of a vehicle as well as the vehicle occupants are schematically represented here. The aim is to capture the proportions of a vehicle using view drawings (side view, cross-section, top view). The position of the individual components such as engine, tank/battery or chassis are roughly coordinated with each other in a first step. In this design, the wheelbase is very wide in order to accommodate additional equipment (e.g., a bicycle).

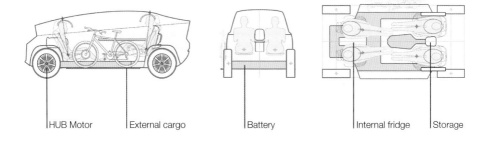

HUB Motor | External cargo | Battery | Internal fridge | Storage

Keysketch rendering

Sketches from the concept phase

In the concept phase, a large number of drawings are created using different techniques. The type of presentation ranges from freehand drawing on paper to digital renderings, which are digitally generated using interactive graphics tablets (Wacom boards). In contrast to renderings on paper, digital renderings offer the possibility of working with many layers. Every line and every shade can be edited to perfection. Within the workflow, it is possible to undo the "undo function", i.e., to undo strokes that have already been drawn. At the end of this phase, the so-called keysketch emerges, in which the formal idea is most clearly visible and forms the basis for the subsequent design phase.

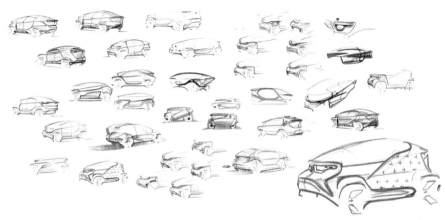

Tape rendering

Tape renderings (side view, half front, rear and roof view) from the selected, best sketches from the concept phase (keysketches) are produced as the basis for a clay model. In the first stage, tape renderings are produced, usually on a scale of 1:4 or 1:5 for cars and 1:3 for motorcycles. In the car industry, however, people often work on a scale of 1:1. This representation technique using fine adhesive tapes allows the design, which is built up in several layers, to be corrected and improved without any problems. The first layer always forms a package drawing, on which the most important assemblies (e.g., engine, tank/battery, chassis) as well as the vehicle occupants are schematically represented. The next layers contain the actual line graphics and the flat shadows or reflections to give the tape rendering a three-dimensional effect.

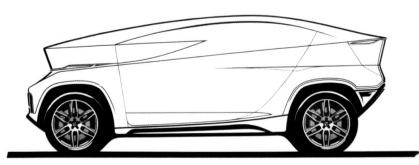

Side view tape rendering

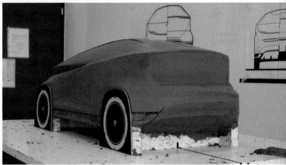

Clay model

The clay model is a model building technique that is mainly used in transportation design. Clay, an industrial plastillin, is applied in layers to a hard foam core (polyurethane). Clay is heated to approximately 56° C in a warming cabinet. This material, which is dimensionally stable at room temperature, becomes soft and can then be applied layer by layer to the polyurethane foam core. Forming is carried out manually by removal using scrapers, stencils or metallic blades. Joint pictures and temporary details are shown on the clay model using removable adhesive tapes.

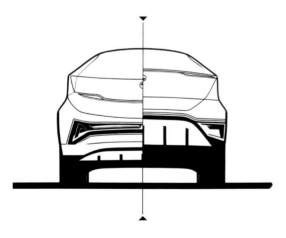

Front view (left) and rear view (right), represented by tape rendering

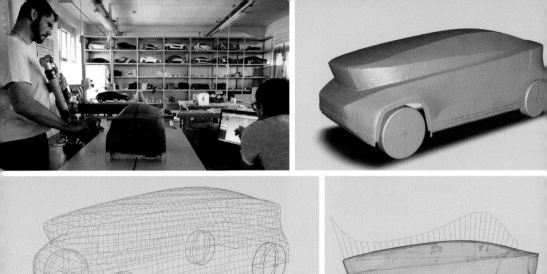

Scanning the clay model

The finished clay model then serves as the basis for the creation of surface data. For this purpose, a virtual model in the form of a point cloud is first created from the real model using contactless scanning systems (stereophotogrammetric systems or laser scanners). In order to obtain a three-dimensional object, these raw data are converted into a polygon model. For better orientation, a set of sections is created parallel to the three main planes. The subsequent development of a three-dimensional surface model is referred to as "reverse engineering".

Editing CAD scan data

To generate surfaces, guide curves are drawn in the plane of symmetry and on characteristic planes and edges. By observing the deviation from the scan data, the curve network is approximated to the scan data by step-by-step adjustment. The curvature is optimized according to design aspects and technical requirements such as maximum and minimum radius or special area characteristics (e.g., barrel areas for side windows) are taken into account. Due to this change in design, feedback loops are introduced between clay model, 3-D scan and reverse engineering, making design development an iterative process. At this point, the design can usually be released on a 1:1 scale.

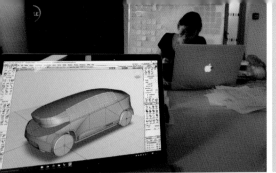
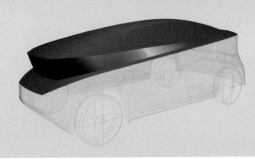

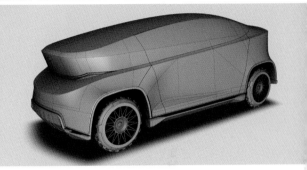

Creating a CAD model

The creation of suitable curves and surfaces requires a great deal of technical and creative understanding and experience. The aim here is to use NURBS geometries (free-form surface data) with as few control points as possible and to select the division of the surface structure according to design and technical specifications. The term "Class-A-model" has established itself in the automotive industry, but there are no standardized criteria for this. However, some characteristics of such surfaces can be generalized, e.g., striving for the lowest possible order, no planar surfaces, only rectangular characteristics of the surfaces, etc.

Alternatively, a polygon model can be generated instead of the surface model, depending on the purpose for which the data will later be used or the design stage of the project.[1]

Milling with a CNC milling machine

The surface model is the basis for a full-scale design model. First, the data is read into a CAM program (Computer Aided Manufacturing). This is followed by programming the milling machine, i.e., selecting the appropriate milling strategies and tools. At the same time, the blank can be cut from PU foam and placed in the installation space. In a simulation, the milling process is checked for surface quality, collisions and efficiency. In design model construction, in contrast to series production, the actual milling time is less important than the time required for programming, since in most cases only individual pieces are produced.

3-D printing

If required, parts from generative manufacturing processes supplement the milled model. These processes build up material layer by layer. Usually these are powder bed, laser sintering, stereolithography or filament processes. What they all have in common is the lack of the required moulds or tools and thus unrestricted shaping. These processes make it possible to manufacture parts from transparent, elastic plastics or metals, for example.

Finish

In order to obtain a representative design model, the parts created and their surface must be completed manually. The finish usually consists of three steps: sanding, priming/fillering and painting. Depending on the model structure, parts are processed separately and are only joined together at the end to form the final model.

 VIMEO video portal of FH JOANNEUM Industrial Design

List of sources:

(1) Bonitz, Peter: Freiformflächen in der rechnerunterstützten Karosseriekonstruktion und im Industriedesign, Verlag Springer, Berlin/Heidelberg, 2009

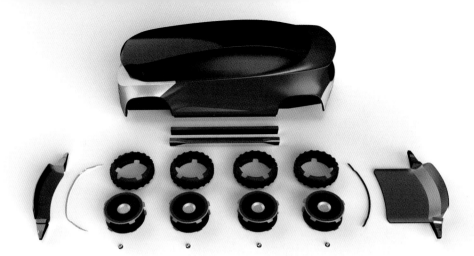

Model M 1:5, single parts (top),
front view (center), rear view (bottom)

Case studies in design

Case studies

Preliminary remarks

The design studies presented in this chapter are practical works by students. Selected project work from the bachelor's and master's studies in Industrial Design at the FH JOANNEUM Graz will be shown.

For the case studies, project works and final theses of a design university were deliberately used, because this offers the following advantages:
The works are not subject to any secrecy and therefore provide a deep insight into the design process and the development work of the students and graduates. As part of the briefing, the work was generally designed for an extended vision horizon of five to 15 years. Most of the case studies were conducted in collaboration with a partner, so that they were closely related to practice. The work was mainly supervised by lecturers who, in addition to their work at the university, also run their own design office. Very often personnel support is also offered by the cooperation partners. Employees from design departments support the university staff from a practical and entrepreneurial point of view.

BMW SAILEFFICIENT

Design and mobility concepts using the example of a speedboat for the BMW brand in 2025.

CASE STUDY 1
SPEEDBOAT BMW SAILEFFICIENT

Master thesis at FH JOANNEUM Industrial Design in cooperation with BMW Group Design
Design: Hans Nikolaus Steen, FH JOANNEUM Industrial Design
Supervisors: Gerhard Friedrich and Felix Staudacher, BMW Group Design
Jürgen Haussmann, FH JOANNEUM Industrial Design

Introduction

The current change in values is a major challenge for mobility providers such as BMW. The trend towards "demotorisation", i.e., away from one's own car towards simple, holistic mobility solutions, calls for new concepts. With its sub-brand BMW i, BMW is already positioning itself as a pioneer of alternative mobility concepts. However, future users, for whom certain innovations have become a matter of course, must be emotionally bound to the BMW brand by new offers and values.

The aim of the work is to design an "event-based" mobility concept in the field of water sports. The BMW-typical brand values are to be transported over these events and to develop a connection to the customer. With the BMW SailEfficient a new "BMW Experience" is generated by the fusion of digital and real contents and thus attention in existing and future target groups is generated. The terms efficiency, dynamics and driver experience, i.e., the typical brand values of BMW, are given special consideration. In the conception of this new concept of mobility, the formal language of BMW is transferred to water sports and expanded. The terms "augmented reality" and "efficiency" fuse together. This means that the events on offer can be experienced as water sports events or passively experienced via social networks and new technologies.

Anology and conclusion in the language of forms

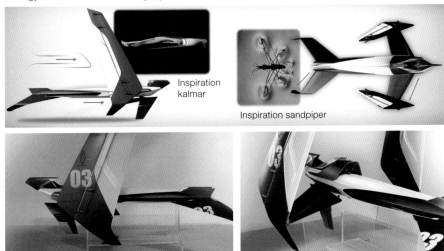

Inspiration kalmar

Inspiration sandpiper

Future scenarios and key factors

The research dealt with the megatrends of the future, the expected change in values and an analysis of the world in 2025, focusing on technical and demographic change and the further development of mobility. Particular attention was paid to sustainability aspects. The most important customer factors that will continue to be decisive for a service provider in the mobility sector in the future were derived from current developments: benefits, comfort, safety, efficiency, added value, experience.

Future developments

In line with the major trends, two aspects of mobility need to be highlighted: On the one hand, "demotorization", the trend away from one's own car towards integrated, simple mobility solutions. On the other hand, car sharing concepts, because a car is only used for an average of one hour a day.

Demotorization

The car as a consumer or luxury good is passé. Mobility and costs are shared wherever possible. A car sharing vehicle can replace 15 private cars. It is estimated that the number of users will rise to over 15 million by 2025 in Europe alone.

Changing values

Your own car is no longer a status symbol: for people under 30, the car is no longer in the top ten of must-haves. This trend is further reinforced by the fact that an automotive brand is less desirable if you don't buy a car yourself. There is hardly any emotional connection to a vehicle if one is basically only interested in the transport from A to B. The result is a more or less emotional connection to the vehicle.

In the future, the automotive industry will increasingly have to contend with a counter-trend caused by a new (non-)buyer group: the trend towards demotorization.

Target audience

The group of persons analyzed for the year 2025 consists of the birth cohorts from 1995 to 2007. The target group is between 18 and 30 years old and primarily interested in innovative media and means of communication. Chat, e-mail and social media are used at all times of the day and night to communicate and report on the respective "whereabouts". Some premium manufacturers, including BMW, are increasingly investing in small cars in order to attract new target groups. Which mobility concepts appeal to the target group outside the automotive environment? Mostly event-based vehicles, such as motor sports vehicles of all kinds. However, it could also be possible to develop fields that relate to the company's history: sailing, airplanes, motor wheels. There are many ways to generate targeted attention.

Problem analysis

The core problem can be defined from the outlined developments:

How can the BMW car brand still be attractive if it no longer touches the user emotionally?

What values should the user associate with the BMW brand in the future?

Efficient dynamics

Safety and security
Intelligent energy management
Technological innovations
Innovative drive technology

Connected drive

Sportiness
Networked vehicle and
infotainment like at home
More comfortable driving and
vehicle handling

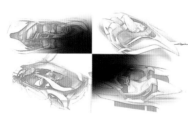

Foundation
Quality
Sustainability
Service
Safety and security
Effectiveness

Emotions
Design
Driving pleasure/joy
Driver orientation
Exclusiveness
Dynamism and elegance

The **BMW brand value** analysis reveals the most essential values such as sustainability, driving pleasure, efficiency, dynamism and elegance.

The resulting question is as follows:

> **What is efficient, sustainable, sporty and conveys a unique driving experience? The "BMW Experience"...**

Concept for water sports

A "BMW Experience" should be efficient, sustainable and agile, but at the same time convey a unique driving experience. These experiences should be formative and influence the brand choice in order to assert oneself in the hard-fought mobility sector. As part of the "BMW Experience", a vehicle concept will be made available at several BMW events or scenarios, which will communicate exactly the values that BMW will stand for in the future. After further research, a vehicle concept for water sports was developed which is used as a "brand shaper" and is particularly convincing for the following reasons:

> Water sports are sustainable, efficient and promote new technologies

> Water sports are safe: the risk of accidents and injuries is low

> New networking approaches: a place for large-scale augmented reality

> Fits into the premium segment without having to be premium

> In Northern Germany, France, Scandinavia, water sports are not elitist

> BMW was already active in the segment (BMW Oracle)

Scenario

A possible scenario is to generate attention via the social networks in accordance with the target group. In the course of an event like the Kieler Woche, the America's Cup or similar, the "BMW Experience" is visited and the concept car is driven or followed during the regatta. The experience is shared and relived on the networks. The values of the BMW brand are thus communicated and henceforth associated with it ("sharing BMW lifestyle") and, as a result, a BMW vehicle may be purchased or DriveNow used ("sharing BMW mobility").

Usage scenario of a "BMW Experience"

Attention is generated by social networks

The event of the "BMW Experience" is visited

In order to be particularly attractive for the target group, it uses net affinity. On the one hand, it is a networked vehicle, which adapts the trend of lifestreaming or "let's play videos". The social environment can experience the "Experience" live, or follow it later. The idea of "gamification" is taken into account through a possible worldwide amateur competition. Using an online platform, the experience can be compared and shared with other users.

Mood board

In a first formal approach to the "BMW Experience" two mood boards are created. Here, the topics "aviation" and "automotive" are brought together in a dynamic collage-like mood board.

Mood board "aviation" (top) and mood board "automotive" (bottom)

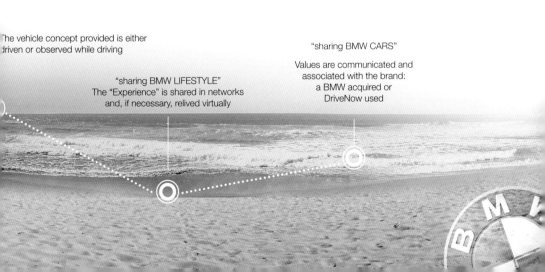

The vehicle concept provided is either driven or observed while driving

"sharing BMW CARS"

"sharing BMW LIFESTYLE"
The "Experience" is shared in networks and, if necessary, relived virtually

Values are communicated and associated with the brand:
a BMW acquired or
DriveNow used

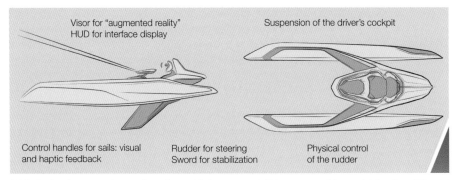

Visor for "augmented reality" HUD for interface display

Suspension of the driver's cockpit

Control handles for sails: visual and haptic feedback

Rudder for steering Sword for stabilization

Physical control of the rudder

A kind of catamaran is used as the vehicle concept. It is powered by a rigid sail or kite, as these are particularly easy to handle and provide sufficient propulsion even with low wind speeds.

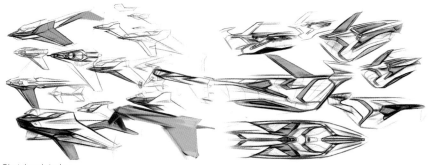

Sketches interior

Sketches exterior

Interior designs

After the master thesis had been written in the interior department of BMW, the interior was also designed. This is related to BMW's current design language. The elevator is controlled by foot pedals and steering levers, which are supported by monitors.

Exploded view and technical parameters

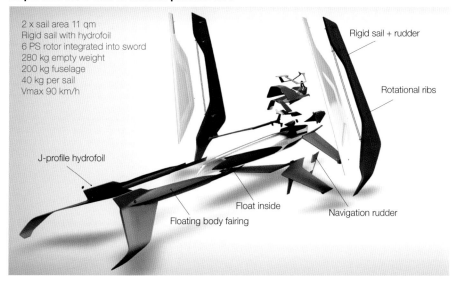

2 x sail area 11 qm
Rigid sail with hydrofoil
6 PS rotor integrated into sword
280 kg empty weight
200 kg fuselage
40 kg per sail
Vmax 90 km/h

Rigid sail + rudder

Rotational ribs

J-profile hydrofoil

Float inside

Navigation rudder

Floating body fairing

Real and virtual use

The digital content for the driver is played back into reality via a kind of head-up display and underlines/supports his driving experience. Similar to a "Redbull Airrace", pylon rides would be conceivable, with the difference that they would only exist digitally. The logistical effort would be much smaller. Additional displays such as passenger position, optimal course, wind window, etc. support the idea of "gamification".

The specially designed interface concept plays with the topic of efficiency. In no other sport is efficiency as decisive as in sailing. This is visualized by means of an instruction and supplemented by a compass. Interlocking geometrics show the degree of efficiency and at the same time give an optimisation recommendation. Theoretically, a transfer to the automotive context can be made at this point.

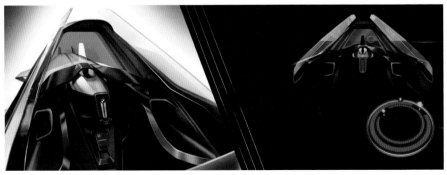

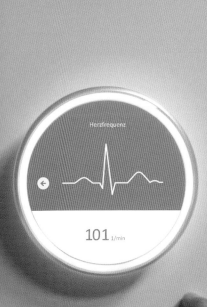

Herzfrequenz

101 1/min

BABY-MONITORING VIA

Design and medical technology using the example of baby monitoring for risk newborns.

CASE STUDY 2
BABY MONITORING VIA
HEALTH CARE FOR RISK NEWBORNS

Master thesis at FH JOANNEUM Industrial Design
in cooperation with Getemed Medizin- und Informationstechnik AG
Design: Christina Wolf, FH JOANNEUM Industrial Design
Supervisor: Johannes Scherr, FH JOANNEUM Industrial Design

Introduction

The birth of a child is a very emotional experience for all parents. After the child has seen the light of day, complications can sometimes occur. Premature births with too low a birth weight and babies with heart rhythm and respiratory regulation disorders are therefore prescribed special health care. In the case of a problematic pregnancy, there is also an increased risk of sudden infant death. Discharge from hospital is therefore a sensitive issue that also raises legal issues. As a precautionary measure, a home monitor (monitoring) of the vital functions in the newborn is consequently ordered by the doctors. If the alarm is triggered at the home monitor, parents can react quickly in the case of a life-threatening condition of the child and must initiate resuscitation measures. Research has shown that the obsolete and very complex application process of the monitor overwhelms many parents. Often a deficient and wrong enrolment is made and too little knowledge is imparted. In daily practice, this leads to frequent false alarms and parents question the usefulness of monitoring.

Approach

A user-friendly home monitoring system, especially for newborns between one and six months of age, should provide the parents concerned with the necessary security in their daily use during monitoring. The further development of the existing product and the revision of the entire usability (operability) will achieve an increased quality level for the monitoring of infants.

Baby monitoring process

Diagnosis: abnormalities in the newborn child ▷ Prescription of a home monitor ▷ Approval of the health insurance ▷ Enrolment in monitor & reanimation course

24h surveillance at home with the monitor ▷ Support by the medical technology company ▷ Continuous evaluation in the hospital ▷ Diagnosis: - remove monitor or - continue

Existing product

2000   **2016**

Research
Mobile phones have evolved rapidly over the past 16 years and smartphones are widely used. The existing monitoring product for newborns has been improved only slightly. Product development should not stagnate, especially in the medical sector.

Market situation and market positioning
There is only a small range of medical devices and most of them are completely outdated and complex to handle. The situation is different for baby monitoring products that are not medically approved. The user-friendliness is largely fulfilled to the fullest satisfaction. What is certain, however, is that these devices cannot be used for therapeutic or diagnostic purposes. They only serve to monitor heart rate, lying position, temperature etc., but do not have an event memory and therefore cannot record or store any episodes which are required for evaluation.

The market analysis has shown that there is little offer for a user-friendly, medically approved baby monitoring system.

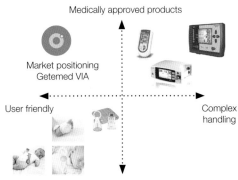

User insights

Interviews with parents, doctors and nurses.

Research has shown that a too complex and outdated application process, i.e., too little know-how, leads to completely overstrained and stressed parents. The understanding for the sense of monitoring their newborn is often lost. It is in the children's interest to take home monitoring to a new level in order to provide them with the necessary protection.

  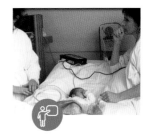

Parents' insecurity

Parents often feel insecure at the beginning of monitoring. Completing a resuscitation course is often difficult and leads to even more uncertainty. What if? Usually the mothers are alone at home with the child. If there is an emergency, action must be taken quickly.

Desensitization

Countless false alarms, always with the same acoustic signal information, lead to an absolute desensitization of the parents. The false alarms are caused by wrong positioning of the sensors, wrong adjustment, releasing the sensor, etc. These aspects are also mostly due to insufficient know-how and can have dramatic consequences.

Handling in everyday life

The handling in everyday life is made more difficult, on the one hand, by the many long cables and on the other hand by the size of the monitor. The design of the device does not offer a flexible application in everyday life. It is very difficult to attach the monitor to the Maxi-Cosi or the crib.

Adhesive sensors

The disposable adhesive sensors used loosen easily and usually have to be fixed additionally. Often the cables themselves cause the sensors to come loose. Attaching the electrodes to the child's upper body by means of an adhesive surface often leads to skin irritations. The environmental aspect of disposable sensors must also be questioned critically.
The dealer has no influence on the consumption.

Know-how

It is a fact that the operating instructions are hardly read by anyone. Parents rely on the pre-programmed, existing settings. These are carried out either by the nursing staff or by an employee of the medical technology company. Due to the unusual situation, it can happen that parents do not record or overlook important instructions for school enrolment.

Complexity

The complexity of the application ranges from the mounting of the sensors to certain monitor settings. Parents are required to schedule a hospital appointment for a 50 percent memory usage so that the evaluation in the hospital does not take too long and the nursing staff can work efficiently.

Product requirements

Simple and uncomplicated operation is required by parents, specialists and dealers and ranges from packaging and monitors to charging stations. Flexibility in everyday life is particularly important for parents. For the newborn, perfect wearing comfort with plenty of freedom of movement is very important. In order to comply with hygiene standards, the devices must be cleaned quickly and easily.

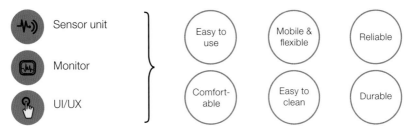

Sensor unit

Monitor

UI/UX

Easy to use

Mobile & flexible

Reliable

Comfort-able

Easy to clean

Durable

Final concept – user journey

If certain abnormalities are de-tected in the child after birth, a home monitor is prescribed.

Parents leave the hospital some-what unsettled on the basis of the diagnosis they have received.

The prescribed monitor is deliv-ered home. Already the pack-aging should leave a positive impression.

A combination of "groundbreak-ing" packaging and digital intro-duction should explain the most important steps.

Step by step, it shows what needs to be done so that no questions remain unanswered and mistakes are avoided.

A pulsating feedback light shows the parents that everything is okay. Display in sleep mode.

The results can only be retrieved by activating the display. Only the feedback light is present.

During the night, the monitor is charged at the charging station. The monitor is in an upright posi-tion, the feedback light is active.

In order to have always charged sensors available, two pieces are delivered in the package.

Elements of the home monitoring system

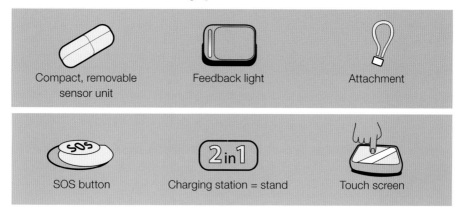

Compact, removable sensor unit

Feedback light

Attachment

SOS button

Charging station = stand

Touch screen

Since pity from "strangers" is not really desired, it is a matter of having an inconspicuous monitor in use.

The data is sent directly to the hospital for evaluation.

If the limit value is exceeded, the sensor sends a vibration impulse to the child, which stimulates breathing.

The monitor must be handy in order to be easy to transport.

One parent leaves the house. The mother knows that if there is an emergency, there is immediate help. Father is informed by the app.

Home monitoring system has an app. The current status of the child can be called up via the app.

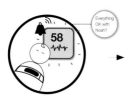

An alarm sounds if the limiting value deviates. In the case of a life threatening condition, the SOS button is used to notify the rescue team.

In emergency situations, resuscitation measures must be initiated (mothers are often stressed). In order to defuse these, there is a signpost on the monitor.

The mother can begin with the rescue measures under guidance and does not lose any valuable time until contact is made with the rescue team.

Design process monitor

The formal design of the monitor deliberately uses round, soft shapes. This appearance is discreetly integrated into the environment of the newborn and the focus remains on the infant. Round shapes symbolically assume the function of a speech bubble. This creates a non-verbal communication about the condition of the child (thought = condition of the baby), which is displayed on the monitor.

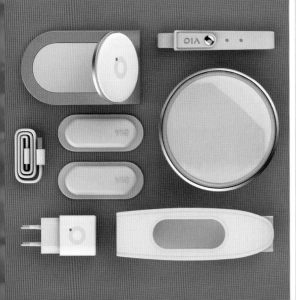

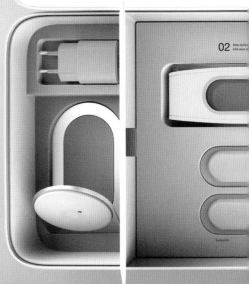

Design process sensor unit

A 100-percent cotton webbing is attached to the child's chest and the monitoring data is transmitted to the monitor via Bluetooth. No more adhesive electrodes are used which could injure the baby's skin and restrict its freedom of movement.

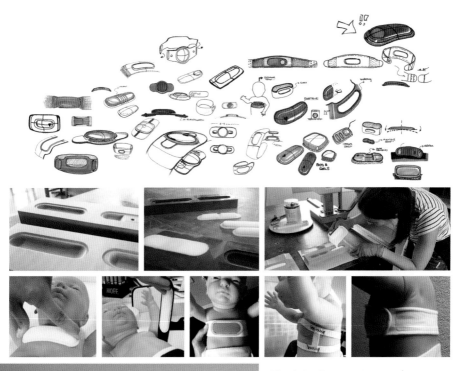

Final design

User-friendliness for parents and child is of paramount importance. With the newly developed sensor technology, a wireless connection to the baby can be established.

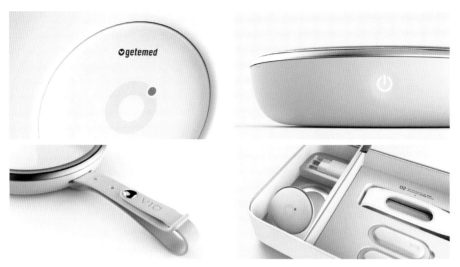

User Interface/user experience UI/UX

Getemed VIA – the new home monitoring system designed specifically for newborns is designed to give parents the confidence they need to monitor their high-risk infant on a daily basis. UI/UX is an essential component of the home monitoring system. The product has been redesigned, starting with the packaging, through the introduction to the handling of the device, to the evaluation of the data. In addition, the intelligent features of the user interface will strengthen the parents' sense of security and ensure professional use in the future.

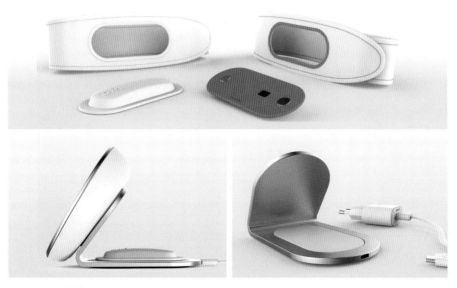

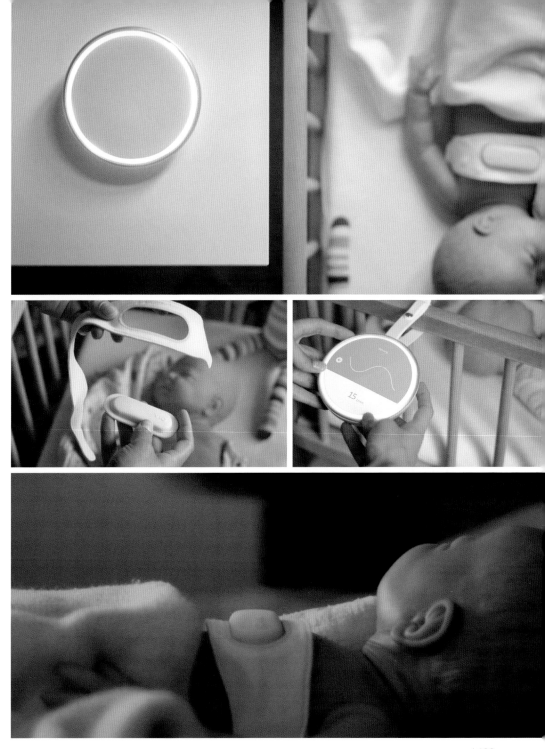

PRINTTEX

Design and innovation using the example of a mobile wall printer.

CASE STUDY 3
MOBILE WALL PRINTER PRINTTEX

Project work with the title "Tooltime" at FH JOANNEUM Industrial Design
Design: Benjamin Loinger, FH JOANNEUM Industrial Design
Supervisors: Johannes Scherr (Design), Matthias Götz (Ergonomics), FH JOANNEUM

Introduction
How can you transfer digital pictures to your own walls? This was the basic question within the semester project "Tooltime" (tools) in 2020. Printtex is a mobile wall printer, which is constructed according to similar technical principles as a standard inkjet printer. The image motif or illustration to be printed on a wall is first generated on a computer or tablet. This is followed by transfer to the Printtex, which is to print the wall. With the help of two sensors, the printing area on the wall is limited. Similar to working with a paint roller, the printer is pulled up and down vertically on the wall.

Innovation

The innovative approach to this product idea is to combine two apparently contradictory products into a completely new product solution. The new product is also extended by various services, such as rent, graphic tool, etc.

The result of the innovation process is the combination of a standard inkjet printer with a paint roller. For the subsequent briefing, however, a number of parameters had to be defined which are decisive for further product development.

MUST

· various print motifs (picture, text, illustration, etc.) are printable
· a paint application that is as even as possible
· a digital input of the print motifs (simple operation)
· the color white should be printable as a special color

TARGET

· independent cleaning of the print heads
· printable on different surfaces (smooth or rough)
· endless printing if required
· the colors are individually refillable

MUST NOT

· the printed image must not smear
· the printer must not tip over during use
· no print offset is to be generated

Product and service

If you want to design the walls of a room yourself with the help of pictures, motifs or texts and do not want to work with complicated projections or templates, proceed as follows:

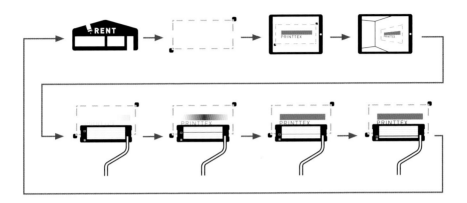

Share

The wall printer can be borrowed from specialist dealers. For the consumer there are no acquisition and storage costs. The borrowed system includes the printer with charging station, five full inkjet ink cartridges and two coordinate sensors. If required, several cartridges can be borrowed. The ink consumption of the cartridges is determined on the basis of the refilled quantity when the cartridges are returned. The refill system saves resources and protects the environment.

Motifs

With Printtex there is no restriction with regard to the selection of motifs. Images, illustrations and texts can be printed. The mode of operation is similar to that of an inkjet printer, whereby white can also be printed on a colored background. Since inkjet printers are based on subtractive color mixing, white must be pre-printed if the wall already has a hue.

Process

Two coordinate sensors limit the pressure range visible on the tablet, laptop or computer. The motif is then placed in the area to be printed and displayed on the screen. The app can be downloaded free of charge from the manufacturer's website. The positioning of the motif can be controlled using a tablet and is displayed in perspective on the recorded livestream. Once the orientation has been determined, the print head must print the respective colors separately. The advertisements on the edge will guide you to the free areas that are still to be printed.

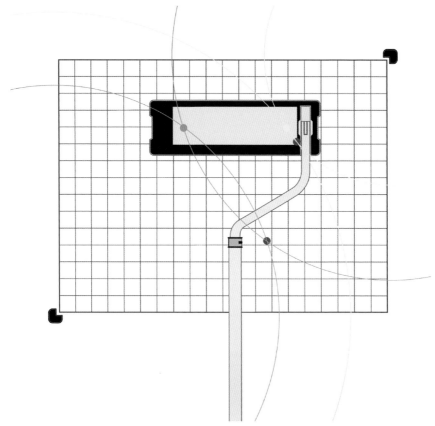

Technical functions

The two coordinate sensors, which diagonally offset limit the pressure range, are connected by infrared. Thus the length of the diagonal can be calculated. A water level is integrated in the print head to prevent confusion of positions. This allows the angle between the straight line and the diagonal to be detected. Each sensor emits two different wavelengths, which hit the two receivers located in the print head. Thus, the position of the print head is always clearly defined.

By changing the position at a certain time interval, the speed at which the wall printer is moved, i.e., the print feed rate, is calculated. Printing ink is applied by rolling over a segment. The sprayed ink density is regulated automatically at a non-constant rolling speed, which is caused by manual operation. A distance sensor for measuring the distance to the wall is installed for checking and securing. If the distance to the wall is incorrect, printing is stopped.

Casing cut

The vertical section through the printer casing shows the required sensors and technical features. The energy is provided by the integrated battery.

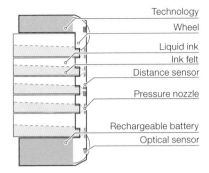

Technology
Wheel
Liquid ink
Ink felt
Distance sensor
Pressure nozzle
Rechargeable battery
Optical sensor

Concept phase

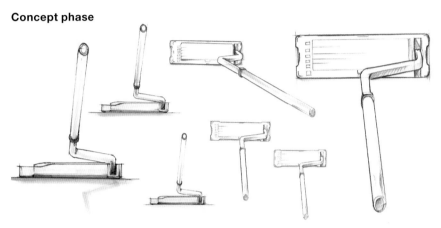

Model making

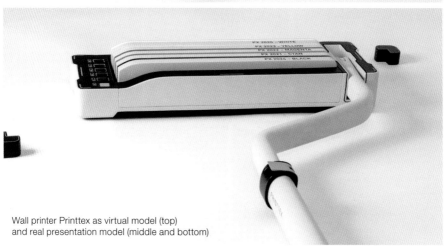

Wall printer Printtex as virtual model (top)
and real presentation model (middle and bottom)

The product was awarded the following prizes:

SCHAEFFLER BALANCE

Design and micromobility using the example of a muscle-powered micromobile with supporting electric drive.

CASE STUDY 4
SCHAEFFLER MIKROMOBIL BALANCE/PROTOTYPE SCHAEFFLER BIO-HYBRID

Project work with the title "Mikromobil" at FH JOANNEUM Industrial Design in cooperation with Schaeffler AG
Design: Isabella Zidek, Joscha Herold, FH JOANNEUM Industrial Design
Supervisors: Michael Lanz, Marc Ischepp, Miltos Oliver Kountouras, FH JOANNEUM

Introduction
In this cooperation project, the students and the Schaeffler Group developed a muscle-powered micromobile with a supporting electric drive. The specification was a slender dimension of 80 centimeters width and a maximum length of 220 centimeters. With a maximum speed of 25 km/h, the vehicle is suitable for cycling on cycle paths and transporting people and loads.

The Schaeffler Group is one of the world's leading integrated automotive and industrial suppliers. Wherever something moves, such as for railways, aircraft, wind power and many other industrial sectors, Schaeffler supplies solutions for the "mobility of tomorrow". By linking industry and mobility, Schaeffler is consistently further developing the micromobility theme. In this context, holistic technical and social considerations play an important role. The cross-border cooperation between this leading German company and FH JOANNEUM Industrial Design was extremely fruitful. This is where the Schaeffler engineers' high level of expertise in the fields of engines, transmissions, chassis and electromobility meets the creative, sophisticated design solutions of the FH JOANNEUM students. This made it possible to further develop the scale model of the design draft into a mobile design prototype.

Design Mikromobil SCHAEFFLER Balance

In the **research phase**, the needs of a potential target group are examined. Special attention is paid to the thorough analysis of future users of a product. This research is carried out by means of personas in which fictitious persons are defined. The interests and wishes of this potential user group will be formulated and further developed in the form of concepts. The persons described do not necessarily have to be the future user groups or consumers, rather they represent a group of potential users with concrete characteristics and user behavior. They assume the role of representatives for various stakeholders.

Persona "post-students"

Munich, center

approx. 25 min

NAOMI
25 YEARS OLD

fashion designer

environmentally conscious
self-confident
athletic
fashion-conscious
in a relationship

elegant

reduced

London, center

approx. 55 min

FRANCIS
36 YEARS OLD

profiler

athletic
trend-/ fashion-conscious
extroverted
single

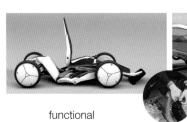

functional

high quality

Part of the research phase is the briefing, with the help of which requirements for the future product are defined in order to be able to develop solutions for these needs in the subsequent concept phase. The wishes of the fictitious persons should be summarized as succinctly as possible (see below) in order to be able to work out the corresponding concepts in further development steps. A good design solution always gives a clear answer to a briefing prepared in advance. The aim is to address the problems and needs of future users in as many ways as possible.

They want...

... to make a statement
... to arrive without sweating
... to take a friend with them
... a work-life balance
... to be physically active

... to save as much time as possible
... to transport shopping
... to take their hand luggage with them
... to arrive dry

Maximum loading volume and storage space

Comfort and weather protection

Drive technology Sporty drive in the smallest possible space and efficient technology

Needs and concepts

... a maximum of comfort and as much storage space as possible
... the space for the drive unit requires as little volume as possible
... sportiness and effectiveness are top priorities when it comes to drive systems
... the target group are active career starters whose center of life is the city center of the future

The transition from the research phase to the ideation or concept phase is usually smooth. In response to the previously defined needs, initial ideas are developed and presented in the form of concept sketches. The CAD software has become more and more user-friendly and this tool is used at a very early stage of the design process. With abstracted 3-D models – supported by simple ergonomics models on a scale of 1:1 – the proportions of the vehicle are roughly determined. Step by step, solutions are fixed and details are worked out in a consistent design process. Modules and assemblies within the overall concept are highlighted in color and spatially positioned (see concept phase below).

Concept phase

Stowing a foldout weather protection in the frame of the vehicle was one of the first ideas in the conception of the micromobile.

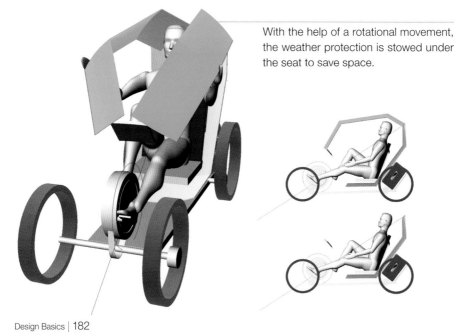

With the help of a rotational movement, the weather protection is stowed under the seat to save space.

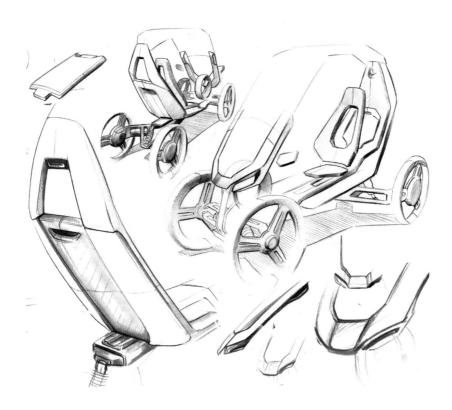

The combination of a one-seater and a two-seater has a decisive influence on the design of the vehicle's frame structure. At the same time, the first tuning of the drive unit takes place. Both the electric drive and a supporting pedal drive must find space within the frame structure.

Design work and dimensions

The structure of the vehicle has been continuously further developed on the basis of the package representations. However, the basis for the CAD design work was the detailed seat studies, which were drawn by hand on paper. The specified external dimensions of the vehicle could not be exceeded. Supporting electric drive units are integrated in the chassis and seat. Steering, light and additional features, such as luggage and emergency seat, are included in the concept, but not yet worked out in detail.

1,500 mm

800 mm

1,350 mm
eye level

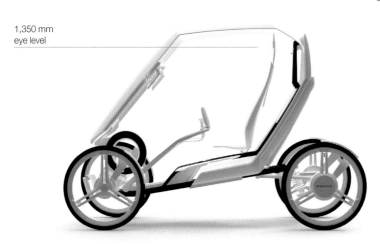

2,200 mm

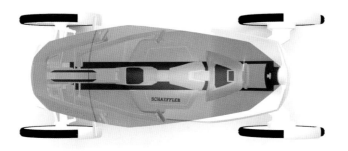

800 mm

2,200 mm

Characteristics

... maximum storage space
... clear panorama
... comfortable sitting position
... free driving experience
... athletic locomotion
... variable weather protection

Parameters of the micromobile:
- 25 km/h maximum speed
- belt drive
- muscle power with
  supporting electric drive
- four wheels

Rotation of the transparent roof cladding

Retractable roof shell for sunny and dry weather

The **Schaeffler Mikromobil Balance** offers a maximum feeling of freedom thanks to its swivelling and stowable weather protection. The integrated and extendable storage space in the rear wall allows objects of different sizes to be transported. In addition, an emergency seat can be folded out to accommodate another person. With the combination of electric drive and muscle power, the user not only makes a contemporary statement, but also finds a compromise between sportiness and comfort.

Closed roof shell for rainy
and cold weather

Cargo bay

Weather protection

Fastening strap, hand luggage

Variable storage space

Second seat folds out

The second seat is a kind of emergency seat,
which is available in case of need

Folding, transparent roof

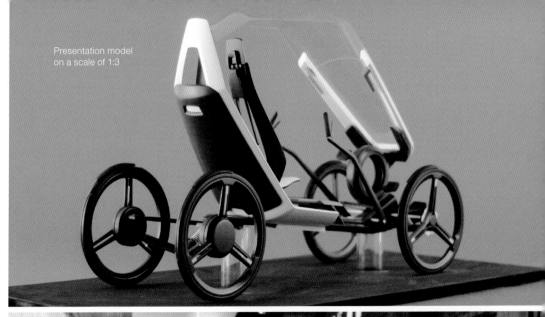

Presentation model
on a scale of 1:3

Schaeffler Bio-Hybrid
From the design model to the driving micromobile in Copenhagen and London

Developing design drafts for series production requires the entire development team to collaborate. The design usually sketches an ideal picture, the further development of which may present designers and engineers with great challenges. In this example, this implementation can be described as extremely successful. The operational muscle-driven micromobile approaches the design from the pen of the students with enormous ease and precision. As so often, it's the details that are most difficult. The question arises as to how slim the chassis can be dimensioned or where the battery can be accommodated with minimal space requirements.

The starting point for this process was the design drafts of the current master graduates of FH JOANNEUM Industrial Design Isabella Zidek and Joscha Herold. Schaeffler, one of Germany's leading industrial and automotive suppliers, together with design experts from designaffairs developed the prototype into a production-ready product.

By integrating existing components, such as disc brakes for bicycles, etc., a CAD design of the vehicle was created (left picture).

The ideas and design language from the design study were consistently implemented. Mechanical components such as the chassis, electrical components (drive/battery) and the development of electronic components (smartphone integration) are parts of this technically very complex vehicle.

Convertible feeling:
retractable roof

Connectivity:
smartphone integration

Automatic gear shift

Portable
battery system

Variable luggage
compartment

Concept

Schaeffler's Bio-Hybrid will combine the advantages of an automobile, e.g., stability and weather protection with the advantages of a pedelec such as lightness, space utilization, and energy consumption. The integration of such lightweight, electrically supported micromobiles into the existing road infrastructure of modern cities is well possible and represents an innovative response to changing mobility patterns. Micromobility can be well developed as a forward-looking concept for locomotion in metropolitan areas and established as an alternative form of mobility. The combination of muscle power with supporting electric drive meets the social trend of a sustainable lifestyle and facilitates the switch to smaller vehicles with a resource-conserving eco-balance. The vehicle impresses with its systemic way of thinking, in which know-how from industry and the automotive sector have been innovatively combined. A diverse development team has succeeded in creating an electromechanical vehicle concept with a forward-looking design language.

Facts and figures

- Bio-hybrid
- Electrically assisted driving (up to 25 km/h)
- Starting aid (boost)
- Range 50–100 km
- Recuperation mode (energy recovery)
- Reverse gear (electric)
- Total weight 80 kg
- Tyres 24 inch

250–750 watt rated power, depending on national legal requirements/target weight 60 kg

1,500 mm

2,200 mm

Flexible weather protection

1+1 seat (child seat)

Ergonomic seat and steering adjustment

From theory to practice in daily use

What was theoretically conceived in a large number of drafts and CAD simulations can be tested for practical suitability in the final test drives in a real environment. Successful test drives were carried out in the bicycle-friendly metropolis of Copenhagen and in the design hotspot London. The basic conditions for future mobility are by no means the same in all regions or nations, but must be viewed in a differentiated way. Depending on regional characteristics, cities such as Berlin or New York can respond differently to people's mobility needs. Especially for flowing bicycle traffic, Copenhagen offers a very dense network of cycle paths separate from the roadway. In London, a narrow micromobile is the ideal answer to escape the ever-increasing traffic jams in the city center without sacrificing comfort. A compact design facilitates the search for a parking space and in many cities there is the right to use the bus lane. Tax relief is a further incentive for a rapid switch to the bio-hybrid vehicle.

Conclusion

The Schaeffler Bio-Hybrid is a proven prototype of a new vehicle type that offers sustainable solutions for the urban mobility of the future.

Testing of the prototype in London and Copenhagen (bicycle-friendly cities)

Test drives in London

MULTI-EQUIPMENT CARRIER EGRA

Eco-Innovative design using the example of an autonomous tool carrier that supports farmers in their work and at the same time protects the soil.

CASE STUDY 5
MULTI-EQUIPMENT CARRIER EGRA

Project: Master thesis at FH JOANNEUM Industrial Design
Design: Helmut Konrad, FH JOANNEUM Industrial Design
Supervisor: Johannes Scherr, FH JOANNEUM Industrial Design

Introduction

This master thesis deals with the topic "Agricultural Work in the Future", with a vision horizon of 15 to 20 years. Agriculture offers a large field of activity, because nowadays almost every agricultural work is supported or automated by the use of machines. At the same time, the process of food production has become very non-transparent for consumers at many farms. Conscious nutrition and organic products are of central importance within society. However, modern agriculture is still influenced by humans and natural environmental factors. One the one hand, yields from farming depend on the location and weather, and on the other hand on the type of farming. The composition of the soil forms the basis for our agriculture. A landscape and environmental protection oriented approach to this cultural asset is therefore of enormous importance for the future. Future generations should also be enabled to practice organic farming.

In the context of the master thesis the following questions were dealt with:
How does the use of machines affect the soil? Is it permanently compatible to use colossal or giant machines? Can today's dominant form of agriculture be described as sustainable?

The equipment carrier designed for use in viticulture and fruit growing as well as for mountainous areas offers an answer to this question. It facilitates the work in agriculture and considers the aspect of soil protection.

Research

Globally, agriculture is an important industry because food production requires a lot of labor. The agricultural machinery used today is very functional, and the technical complexity is very high. There is a lot of development work involved in these machines in order to ultimately be marketable and to meet the requirements of the customer. The quality of the design has strongly influenced these machines in recent years and manufacturers are looking for innovative design solutions.

In the context of an intensive research on the subject of agriculture the damage caused by the use of machines on the ground is analyzed and new approaches to solutions are sought. This valuable information forms the basis for the development of a scenario from which the design concept is derived and innovative solutions are created.

$$\text{PRESSURE} = \frac{\text{POWER}}{\text{SURFACE AREA}}$$

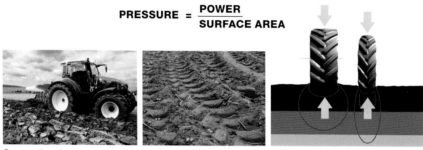

Compaction due to excessive wheel loads and ground pressure

The research shows that excessive wheel loads on agricultural machinery cause enormous damage to fertile soils. At the same time, there is a trend towards almost complete automation in agricultural machinery and the dimensions of these machines are also constantly increasing. Another trend is the cultivation of partial areas by so-called field robots and drones. Historical retrospect shows that fewer and fewer people are being used to cultivate agricultural land.

Industrialization and increase in mechanization

Mass & size

| 500 BC | Mid-19th century | Today | Future |

Effects of industrialization on agricultural machinery

Several surveys were carried out on the subject of soil protection and areas of application for agricultural machinery. The group of persons included experts for cultivation equipment and viticulture as well as the head of the Institute of Agricultural Engineering of the University of Natural Resources and Life Sciences in Vienna. The following aspects were derived from these discussions:

- **Limiting the mechanical load**
- **Adaptation of working methods**
- **Use of technical innovations**

Two scenarios were examined for the creation of the design concept. The scenario 2025 "E-volution" deals with the increase of storage capacities of batteries and offers a high innovation potential for the development of agricultural engineering. Industrialized agriculture has left many scars on our planet, affecting vast landscapes and valuable land. Now is the time to start a counter-trend.

The more comprehensive scenario 2034 "the green turnaround" is a first step in this direction. An existing trend is being reinforced, leading to an about-face – increased demand for organic products combined with transparent and deliberately sustainable food production. Novel agricultural systems considerably support the farmer, making him a sustainable producer within a process chain.

The values for the "green turn" include the following aspects:

- **Deceleration and balanced interaction between people and technology**
- **Preservation of the landscape as well as ecological and regional production**
- **Family in the center of life and conscious and healthy lifestyle**

At the end of the research phase, the vehicle concept is defined and the target group selected. The focus is on winegrowers, fruit growers and farmers who work in mountainous areas and need machinery that can be adapted to the terrain.

The objective is to support and relieve people in their work in agriculture and to minimize the potential danger.

Inspiration and guiding principle for the vehicle concept is an autonomous and modular equipment carrier platform. The steep terrain with narrow tramlines and often bumpy access roads predominates in viticulture, fruit growing and mountain farming. These topographical requirements must not be an obstacle for the machines used. The design briefing was prepared with these special requirements in mind. This specification catalog is also an important aid for the creation or dimensioning of the vehicle package.

With regard to topography, the following requirements apply:

flat terrain	steep terrain	narrow paths
for use on the plain and fields	for use on mountain farms or in viticulture	on access to exposed slopes or between vines

The main objectives of the briefing were:

MUST	TARGET	MUST NOT
· work with soil protection · be able to drive autonomously · flexible use · stable on slopes · compact form · transporting goods, working the soil and plant care · simple attachment · clear advantage over a tractor	· monitor the fields and plants · relieve and support the farmer · be environmentally friendly in operation and maintenance	· destroy the soil · pose a threat · endanger people and animals

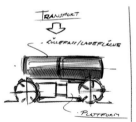 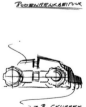 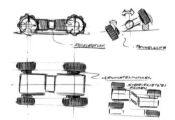

The following relevant details for package creation were fixed taking into account the factors listed:
· wide tyres and double tyres
· tape drive
· lightweight construction with technology in the substructure
· modular system and compact design
· motor and quick coupling system for attachments
· liquid manure barrel, syringe application or loading area
· a flying drone collects important data during work deployment and serves to monitor and control the equipment carrier
· exclusively electric drive systems

The briefing provides a clear objective, which is the development of a flexible, modular and autonomous equipment carrier in combination with a drone that fulfils analysis and monitoring functions.

Concept

In the first sketch phase, fundamental considerations were made about the package. The starting point was the equipment carrier platform, on which different modules can be mounted. It was important to consider the functional requirements from the briefing on the one hand and to define a design that harmonizes with the entire product range on the other.

During the first sketch phase, a CAD package is created that is very helpful for checking the various steering options and roughly defines the dimensions of the machine. At the same time, the volume of existing equipment carriers from similar areas of application is used for comparison. These first computer-supported package displays also served as underlay for the further design sketches. As a result, the design became more and more concrete and elaborated using CAD software (SolidWorks/Alias). The SolidWorks volume modeler was very helpful for the technical components, because solid bodies can be created relatively easily with this software. A surface modeler (Alias) was used to work out the outer enveloping surfaces.

 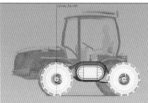 

CAD package representations

Equipment carrier with wheel hub motors   Inspection of the steering angle (tape drive)

At the beginning of the design development, the focus was on the conception of the equipment carrier platform, which is driven by four wheel hub motors with battery support. It is equipped with all-wheel steering and a pendulum axle to adapt to different terrain conditions and keep ground pressure low. This is followed by the development of the main module, the equipment carrier. In terms of materiality, natural fibre composites characterize the design language of Egra. When modeling the main module and the attachments, a uniform design language was taken into account. Thus a consistent and coherent design language could be realized.

Formal reference Steyr diesel tractor

Main module

Modules for slurry

Modules for slurry, harvest, viticulture and transport

Modules for harvesting, viticulture, crop protection and liquid manure

Equipment carrier (below) and the drone (above)

Furthermore, a plant protection, slurry and harvesting module as well as a drone complete the Egra concept. With the aid of the drone, the farmer can monitor the work and carry out the navigation. In order to get a realistic impression of the different modules in the area of operation, photomontages were made. They show the add-on modules during different agricultural activities.

Conclusion

Egra, the electric, fully autonomous and modular equipment carrier, is a trend-setting product for agriculture that allows a significant increase in working efficiency in agriculture. Due to the modular system, the aspect of soil protection is taken into account. The product-like design language offers a high degree of functionality and supports the high degree of innovation. Formally, elements from the transport design and traditional elements of tractors are combined into a compact unit.

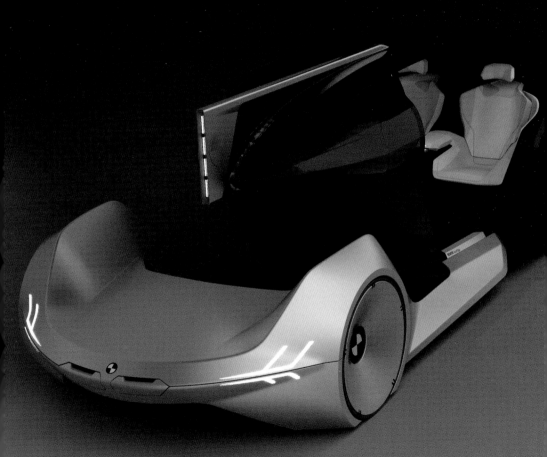

BMW AURIGA

Design and automated driving using the example of an automotive vehicle for BMW.

CASE STUDY 6
BMW AURIGA AUTOMATED DRIVING 2030

Project work FH JOANNEUM Industrial Design in cooperation with BMW Group Design
Exterior design: Philipp Fromme; interior design: Daniel Brunsteiner, Florian Howecker,
FH JOANNEUM Industrial Design
Supervisors: Gerhard Friedrich and Christian Bauer, BMW Group Design
Michael Lanz, Marc Ischepp and Miltos Oliver Kounoutras, FH JOANNEUM Industrial Design
Walter Lach, Petrus Gartler, Miltos Oliver Kountouras (model making), FH JOANNEUM

Task
Automated driving is an important topic for BMW as well as for all other car manufacturers. Automatic control of vehicles will massively influence the design of the interior, as the demands and free spaces of passengers will change dramatically.

The following questions were therefore important for BMW: How can BMW's brand values be staged in an automatically driving vehicle, both in the exterior and in the interior, in such a way that they are credible and recognizable on the one hand and attractive for BMW's various target groups on the other? In the first phase of the project, it was important to analyze user behavior, define target groups and develop clear user profiles based on personas. In the subsequent concept phase, the aim was to tell "stories" and succinctly present the functional and emotional qualities of the vehicle study. The vehicle concept was then developed on the basis of a full-scale tape rendering and the final esthetics of the concept were created. The concept studies were then worked out as a scale exterior model.

Concept
In a future of uniform shared mobility, BMW needs a flagship that offers personal premium mobility and picks up and reinterprets the brand values of joy and dynamism. The visual analogy of a draft horse makes the dynamics and independence of the vehicle visible to the outside world. A clear separation of the passenger compartment creates a new, luxurious feeling of space. The joy of owning the BMW Auriga is enhanced by the vehicle's intelligence, which gives the user new freedom.

Carriage and draft horse

Development of the BMW model family

The effects of this scenario on the BMW product family are illustrated in the graphic below. Models 1, 2 and 3 will become a "shared" vehicle that will have approximately the same dimensions as the current BMW i3. The sporty 4 Series and 6 Series models would be combined into a semi-autonomous sports car to appeal to sports enthusiasts. The higher-class models of the 5 Series and 7 Series will eventually be replaced by the BMW Auriga, making it the autonomous luxury vehicle of the future.

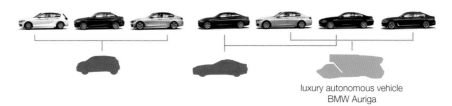

luxury autonomous vehicle
BMW Auriga

Trend research

Trend research shows a clear direction that cars will drive autonomously in the near future. This means that shared mobility will be cheap and therefore very attractive. In this world of 2030, which is dominated by generic, autonomous vehicles, there is a need for a flagship that represents the BMW values. Shared mobility requires a vehicle that brings back the joy of owning a car and creates added value for the user.

"A day in a life" personas and target group definition

In order to design a vehicle that would meet the needs of the target group, personas had to be developed and a day in the lives of these people had to be gone through. This results in corresponding wishes and requirements.

Hachirou Yuuta Minami
Age 34
Nationality London, UK

Profession: fashion designer

BMW moment
Get inspired
Connect with people
Amazed

BMW moment
Creative
Design studio
Enthusiastic

Photo studio
Creative director
Impulsive

BMW moment
Writing articles,
posting pictures

Conference
Negotiate

Work on collection
Define, create

BMW moment
Fashion studio
Accomplish, thinking

Rest
calm, enjoy

Roots of luxury mobility (research)

In order to fathom the roots of luxury mobility, the history of the automobile was analyzed. Luxury vehicles of that time all had one thing in common: the driver of the vehicle was not necessarily the driver. At that time this insight brought the chauffeur of a vehicle as the first source of inspiration to the fore.

The roots of the automobile date back to horse-drawn carriages. The horse as a driving force has certain similarities with the way autonomous vehicles work. It is intelligent enough not to get off the road and takes countermeasures to avoid accidents. The only input the driver has to provide is direction and speed.

Analogy: In the research phase, the origins of mobility were investigated, which in turn had a strong influence on the concept. The chauffeur-driven carriage was the preferred means of transport of the affluent class for a long period of time. It combines the comfort of a separate cab with the combined intelligence of the driver and the draught horse.

The chauffeur...   and the carriage

Create added value

By assisting BMW Auriga with everyday tasks, valuable time is freed up that can be used for other important things in life. This way of making life easier and more efficient for the owner are the future "BMW joy" moments. BMW Auriga can do many tasks independently and organizes them according to the owner's schedule. The vehicle can use unoccupied time to complete tasks such as picking up family members or getting groceries from the shop.

Interior layout

The interior of the BMW Auriga should adapt to the different driving situations in which the owner can find himself. The graphic below shows four possible scenarios in which the interior of the vehicle adapts accordingly. These adaptations are to be achieved with as little hardware modification as possible in order to allow smooth transitions.

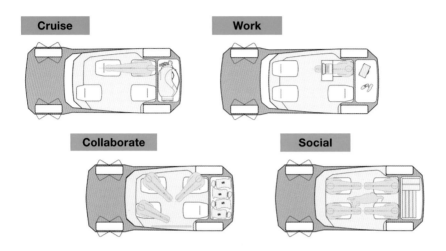

Interior scenarios

Innovative functions and concepts were developed to implement these different scenarios in the interior. Brainstorming sessions were used to generate ideas, evaluate them and put them on paper using small "thumbnail sketches". Scenarios such as relaxation zones with music, multimedia projections, parties, gaming and many other ideas were visualized.

Benchmark and package

Data and dimensions of existing vehicles were subjected to a comparative analysis in order to develop the proportions of the BMW Auriga. In order to simultaneously achieve the largest possible interior dimensions as well as the best possible aerodynamics and efficiency, a form factor similar to that of the Mercedes F 015 concept was chosen. The exterior dimensions of the BMW Auriga are roughly the same as those of the BMW 7 Series.

2015 Mercedes F 015 Concept
Electric Hydrogen Hybrid
SIMILAR INTERIOR CAPACITY

EXTERIOR HARDPOINTS

Lenght	5,220	4,600-5,000
Width	2,018	2,100
Height	1,524	1,490
Wheelbase	2,610	3,025-3,425

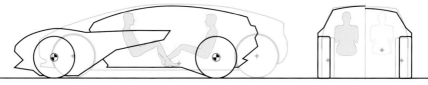

In order to check the proportions of the vehicle, a 1:1 mockup of the interior was built.

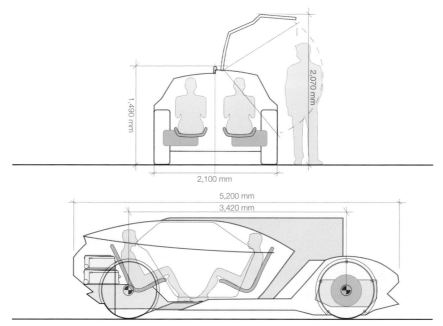

Sketch phase exterior

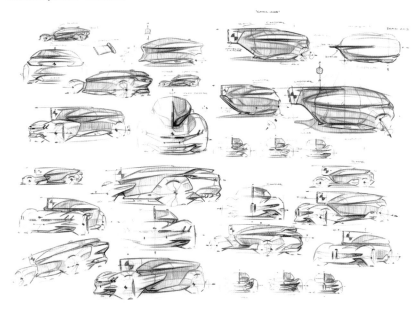

Exterior

The drawings developed more and more from traditional vehicle designs towards an autonomous driving experience. The focus was clearly on an autonomous outer appearance, supported by simple and clear lines. In addition, emphasis was placed on giving the vehicle as much lightness as possible while still achieving maximum volume. The in-depth design work was carried out using Photoshop renderings with clear lines.

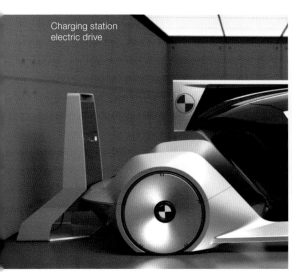

Charging station electric drive

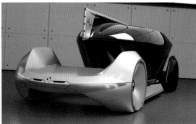

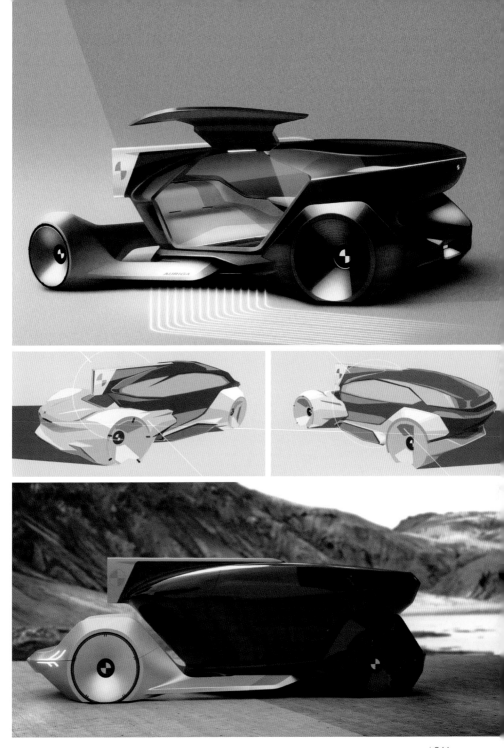

Sketch phase interior

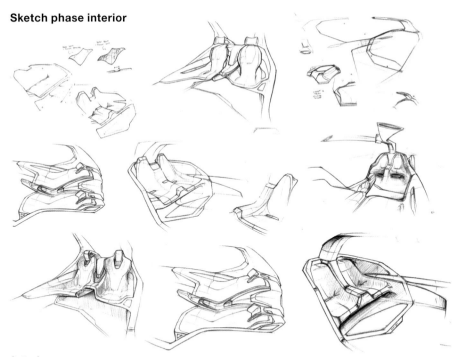

Interior

A luxurious yet versatile interior is the central design theme here. Leather seats in an optimum seating position provide an overview and a special comfort experience. The seats can be transformed into different states. Depending on requirements, you can switch from "work mode" to "lounge mode".

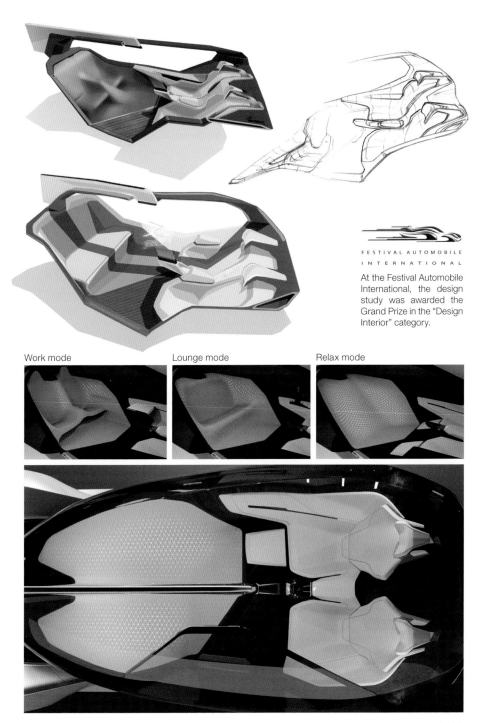

FESTIVAL AUTOMOBILE
INTERNATIONAL

At the Festival Automobile International, the design study was awarded the Grand Prize in the "Design Interior" category.

Work mode

Lounge mode

Relax mode

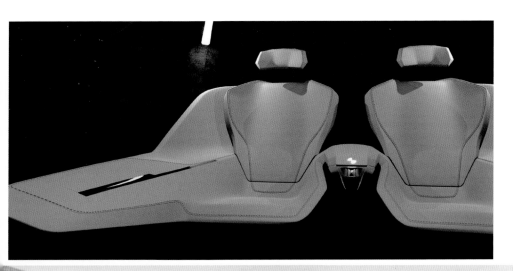

Video or animation on www.vimeo.com
https://vimeo.com/user63132342

SAILPLANE NORTE

An electrically powered glider with a focus on safety and usability.

CASE STUDY 7
SAILPLANE NORTE

Master thesis at FH JOANNEUM Industrial Design
Design: Alexander Knorr, FH JOANNEUM Industrial Design
Supervisor: Johannes Scherr, FH JOANNEUM Industrial Design

Introduction
Gliding is one of the niche sports and has about 107,000 pilots worldwide. This sport is mainly practiced in clubs that have been suffering from membership loss for years. The aim of this master thesis is to inspire young people to fly gliders.

Norte is a two-seater glider with an integrated electric motor, which enables a self start. With the help of a bipod landing gear, the glider pilot can take off alone without further assistance. The economical use is based on a sharing system, which offers many advantages to independent pilots (without club membership), but also to clubs. Access to aircraft should be as easy as possible in order to attract more interested parties to aviation. A look at the accident statistics and the currently used safety systems required a fundamental revision and improvement of the construction and technology of the glider pilot. The safety concept now includes several active and passive safety systems that offer the pilot optimum protection. In addition, the user experience has been redesigned to provide pilots with a novel flying experience, with special emphasis on safety aspects during flight and landing.

The statistics show a decrease in accidents, but the number of fatal accidents remained approximately the same. The decrease in the number of accidents can also be partly attributed to the decrease in licenses.*

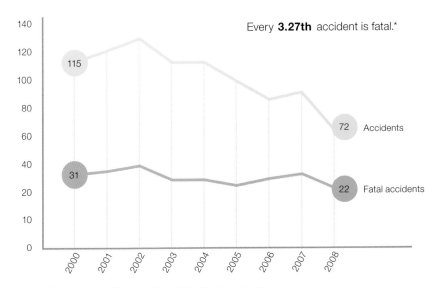

Source: German Federal Bureau of Aircraft Accident Investigation

Problem

Gliders are very often involved in accidents according to the accident reports of the German Federal Bureau of Aircraft Accident Investigation. It is astonishing, however, that more fatal accidents occur in this context than with other aircraft. This is mainly due to the way gliders fly. Conventional microlight or motorized aircraft are not dependent on thermal conditions and therefore do not enter dangerous situations as often as gliders.

Types of accidents in gliding:

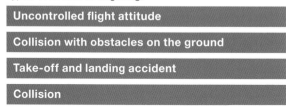

Uncontrolled flight attitude

Collision with obstacles on the ground

Take-off and landing accident

Collision

Gliding clubs worldwide are suffering from a loss of members. In the last eleven years, the number of gliding licenses has decreased by 16.36 percent. In the two largest sales markets, the USA and Germany, the percentage is even higher and tends towards -20 percent. The average age of the members is rising. Reasons for this are a high leisure offer, the resulting costs for the receipt of the license and the large expenditure of time as a member in the association.

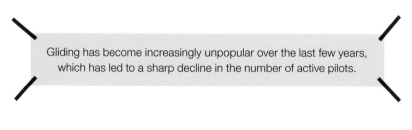

Gliding has become increasingly unpopular over the last few years, which has led to a sharp decline in the number of active pilots.

Decline in licenses worldwide

-16.36 % Number of licenses
2001–2012

Reasons for this are:

Costs	Expenses	Unattractive
Gliding is expensive compared to other sports.	Due to the structure of the clubs, a lot of time has to be invested in the sport.	There is an oversupply of leisure activities.

Sharing system

Clubs buy their flying machines in the group, which are mostly paid for out of the club's coffers. New prices are between 120,000 and 160,000 euros (depending on equipment and provider). However, there is a large second-hand market where glider pilots are offered from 12,000 euros. In addition to the existing aircraft fleet of a club, a Norte glider is purchased. This airplane is used by club members like an airplane of the club, in addition, non-members can fly with it. Non-club pilots book the aircraft for a certain time window and the club earns additional income due to higher minute costs.

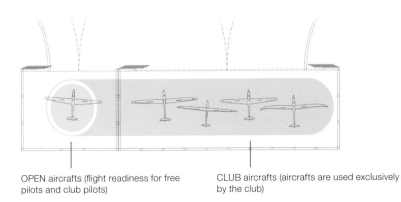

OPEN aircrafts (flight readiness for free pilots and club pilots)

CLUB aircrafts (aircrafts are used exclusively by the club)

Advantages for clubs and pilots

Additional income for the association

The operation of such planes brings additional money into the association's coffers and helps to finance new acquisitions more easily.

Proximity to potential new club members

Pilots who regularly use the service automatically come into contact with the club due to local conditions and could transfer to the club.

Pilot only pays for performance

Membership fees are not due, because one invests in pure flight time. For pilots with medium to few flying hours and beginners it is a very profitable model.

More time in the air

There are no club hours to be done. So the pilot spends more time with flying and not with club affairs.

Promotion of gliding tourism

Besides partner associations, club members can also make use of airplanes in regions without club connections.

Core elements exterior

Folding propellers
To reduce drag, the propellers can be folded and parked in bays.

Replaceable batteries
The system is equipped with replaceable batteries to ensure continuous operation. This means that charging times can be better clocked and the aircraft can fly more hours.

Long safety cell
Enlarging the safety cell generates more space which can serve as a crumple zone.

Crumple zone
In the event of a crash, the first impact is absorbed by a crumple zone. The slanted separation of parts helps to reduce the impact energy.

Bipod chassis
In order to ensure uncomplicated take-off and landing, the concept uses a bipod chassis. No further help is needed for take-off.

In the **concept phase**, many technical functions, which are referred to here as core elements, were shown schematically. These considerations became part of the package drawing and were subsequently incorporated into the design draft.

Package of a conventional self-starter

Ground Starting Position

Safety cell	EM 42
Lithium-ion batteries – 12 moduls 160 A	Diameter: 250 mm
Rescue system	Length: 272 mm
Water ballast	29.12 kg
FES – 42 kW	42 kW

Core elements interior

Floating dashboard
A free-hanging dashboard gives the pilot more space. It also enables taller pilots to get in and out comfortably and generates more legroom during the flight.

Safety tub
Due to hygiene requirements, the tub is designed to be easy to clean. No components are fixed directly to the floor, creating a continuous surface.

Seat suspension
Damage to the spine can be caused by hard contact. To prevent these injuries, the seat is suspended on two points and can absorb moderate blows.

Small instrument panel
The instrument panel is reduced to the most necessary instruments (trip meter, variometer, speedometer, compass and altimeter) to facilitate getting in and out.

Augmented reality
With augmented reality support, flight data can be projected into the pilot's field of vision and other features support navigation, adapted to the respective situation.

By comparing the Norte concept with a conventional self-launcher, the changed technical structure is clearly visible. The features developed as core elements become integral components of the glider pilot.

Package of the Norte concept

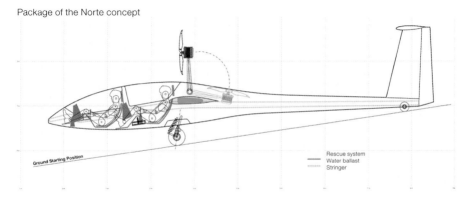

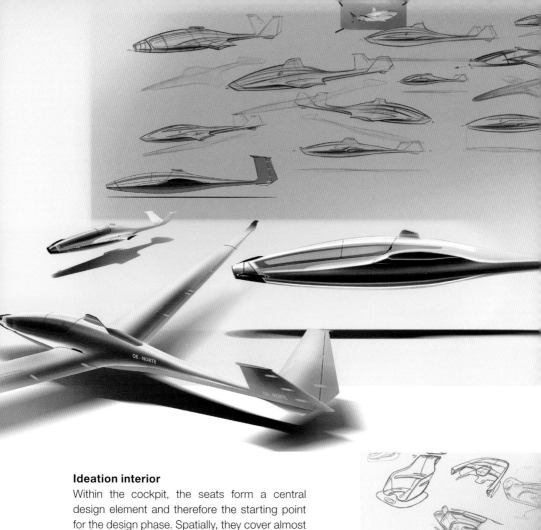

Ideation interior

Within the cockpit, the seats form a central design element and therefore the starting point for the design phase. Spatially, they cover almost the entire cockpit, which is also surrounded by the frame as a central element. All movable parts are connected to this frame and pilots of different body sizes can be seated in the cockpit. The suspension of the seats provides damping, which can absorb forces in the event of a hard landing or impact.

Ideation exterior

Due to the physical laws of nature, gliders are severely restricted in their design. Therefore, it also plays with elements of the nature of our water world. As a source of inspiration, the shark, which moves particularly efficiently in the water, came to the fore. The design features of the shark were transferred to the aircraft, which are particularly reflected in the bulbous front and the fin.

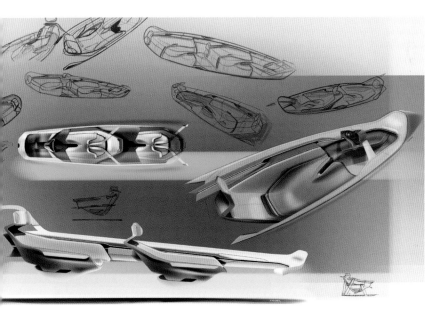

Three-bladed folding propeller

Due to the three propeller blades, the drive is more powerful and less subject to vibration. This improves the flight behavior and reduces the susceptibility of the propulsion system. The diameter of the propeller can be smaller and achieve the same performance as a two-bladed propeller, which is currently standard.

Longer cockpit

The muzzle serves as impact protection and a predetermined breaking point to prevent the aircraft from digging into the ground in the event of a crash.

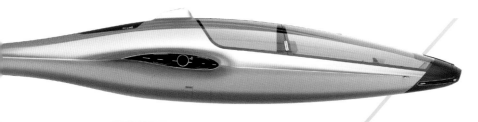

Foldable propeller

Replaceable batteries

Bipod chassis

Seat suspension

Norte is a two-seater that can be controlled from both seating positions. This aircraft can thus be used for training purposes and flights with passengers. In order to adapt the seating position to the different sizes of the occupants, in addition to the seat shells, the pedals for the elevator and the headrests can also be adjusted. At the front seat, the dashboard can be moved to facilitate boarding. The seating position of the rear pilot is slightly raised to give the second pilot a good overview.

Section through the cockpit

Shock absorbing seats

Supporting interface

Seat layout – two-seater

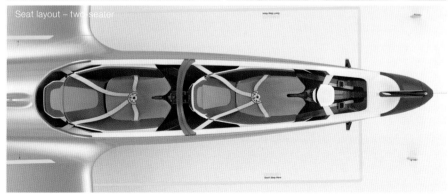

Video or animation on www.vimeo.com
https://vimeo.com/user63132342

Development perspectives in design

Outlook

Development perspectives of design and innovation in the context of big data and increasing complexity

A reliable *view into the future* is an old dream of mankind. The desire for precise predictions affects different areas of life: the "reading" of one's own future and that of others, the future of one's own discipline and society, the development of one's own securities portfolios and the economy as a whole.

The desire for *predictability of the future* (e.g., through forecasts that are as accurate as possible) is beyond serious access due to the complex characteristics of our society's systems. Nevertheless, once we have understood the corresponding system laws and have trained and applied the necessary processes and methods, we are able to understand possible future *development patterns* (in the truest sense of the word in all possible accessible sensory levels). This is precisely one of the strengths of *design* and *industrial design*. Not only disciplinary, i.e., in product development, but also as the integration of all available levels of perception as the necessary interface between different disciplines and actors in the sense of a necessary cross-border knowledge integration (note: for this purpose it is also necessary to fill often existing empty words with substance, for example the often superficial use of methodical concepts such as "design thinking").

The hope of being guided by almost unlimited amounts of data as if by an invisible hand (= algorithms) and then automatically being able to read future developments is certainly a myth. With regard to an increasing *"big data hype"*, it should be noted that more data ("big data") without having understood the connections and – above all – without having asked the "right" questions and carried out the appropriate analyses, is just as misleading. The "superstition" of being able to meet the great challenges of our society through reductionist, single-disciplinary silo solutions that negate society's expertise is not conducive to success. Or in other words – big data is simply a lot of data and when processed in erroneous analysis procedures, it inevitably results in erroneous results, whereas its true potential lies in the application of appropriate analysis methods and processes, as well as sophisticated data design.

An *"intelligent and successful"* expedition group, for example, will not only embark headfirst on an adventure and then most likely suffer "shipwreck", but will also prepare itself for this adventure and any "surprises" associated with it in a scenario-oriented manner. In order to be optimally equipped for the "future" adventure, a bundle of competencies is required that go far beyond the skills that have been written up to now. For the complex challenges of today and tomorrow, designers and *problem-solvers* increasingly need sociocultural, personal and systemic competences in combination with comprehensive specialist competences (depending on the given task) in addition to the classical skills and creative competencies associated with the job description. This is also the case, for example, with regard to the previously mentioned goal-promising, successful and responsible handling of "big data".

Innovation as deep snow downhill run

However, forecasts concerning the emergence of *new technologies* (and the ability to interpret their signs at an early stage) and major *societal transformations* are of general interest and, of course, particularly relevant to the areas of design and innovation: the term "technology" refers, for example, to the possibilities of generating whole buildings, rocket propulsion systems (currently already implemented at NASA), earthquake-proof houses (successfully used in China for houses that are still safe in earthquakes up to 8.0 on the Richter scale) or human organs and other body parts (in the foreseeable future) in 3-D printing and the associated consequences in all areas of life; however, the signs for this technology go back to their original development by Charles Hull in 1983. When we think of "social transformation", we think of a possible international political reorganization or increasing population growth, but also poverty traps in Africa or an unprecedented migration movement due to climate change (and not because of a new political trouble spot). Understanding these basic "big" patterns affects all other areas on a meta-level, including design and innovation. And it is often innovation that, in many of these areas of change mentioned above, as an intervention mechanism, represents the possibility of being able to meet these great present and future challenges (i.e., also the risks and vulnerabilities and not only the opportunities offered by new market potentials) and – ultimately – to contribute to an increase in the resilience of our society as well as to sustainable development in general. The following diagram is an overview of these challenges, the so-called Global Grand Challenges presented as current "Sustainable Development Goals" of the UN.

The major current and future challenges facing society

The essential bridge to the future for (industrial) design is innovation. With this the only way to address the question of development perspectives in design is by linking them to innovation, innovation and design processes, as well as innovation systems and the actors directly and indirectly associated with them (the understanding of users, but also of various other stakeholder groups and not to forget the understanding of the motivations of non-users).

Considerations regarding the future of design require a broader perspective. In the past, disciplinary and product-focused approaches were promising. However, increasing networking and globalization have not only led to closer economic ties, but have also affected all levels of society: social media have now been used to define and expand "friends" across the globe, but they have also increasingly watered down the concept of friendship. Employment relationships are often determined by functional and topic-specific activities, whereby institutional assignment is often more difficult, because the importance of institutional multiple assignments ("affiliations") is rising to an increasing extent. What is valid in the world of work, however, also has an effect on our life worlds – on the one hand, physical and virtual mobility makes more and more different value and social systems accessible to us, but at the same time, the mechanisms of value system affiliation and identity formation are also changing. The exponentially increasing intensity of the effects of digitalization opens new doors and possibilities for development on a private, professional, industrial and political level, but also shakes the pillars of our own understanding, especially in the sense of coupled human-machine systems and the self-organization mechanisms behind them, feedback and amplification mechanisms, as well as the associated risks and vulnerabilities (the basic considerations of the basic principles of cybernetics articulated in the middle of the last century seem to be of utmost importance for the understanding of these functional mechanisms, especially today and for the future). For the much sought-after understanding of future developments, valid (deterministic) prognosis models have recently lost their truth content, which shows the necessity of understanding complex development patterns (only a few areas of science are prepared for these challenges).

Today, the increasingly complex tasks in a dynamically changing world require a broader perspective that transcends disciplinary boundaries. For this reason, some central thoughts in dealing with an uncertain and complex future will be presented below, followed by a design-specific consideration. The main focus here is on potentially extended future areas of design, for example, in the form of strategic overall developments.

General and global future development paths are not only related to future orientation, forecasts, trends and visions. These often become visible when one deals with historical developments because they have led to where we are today – with all their sunny and dark sides. Especially current undesirable developments that have led not only to a financial disaster but also to a crisis in society as a whole, such as the nuclear catastrophe in Fukushima, Japan, in 2011, associated with an earthquake and a tsunami, or the refugee crisis in Europe from 2015, clearly show a general need for action in social developments and thus in our thinking. This affects a wide range of our activities, including those of design. In the turbulences of everyday life, one runs the risk all too quickly of only reacting, not acting. We tend to look for "signs" for future developments that can also turn out to be "false" beacons. The basic conditions of this action with their multiple interactions are often not examined in depth and the principles of thinking and working together are insufficiently questioned. Today, however, we also offer unprecedented opportunities by replacing the mirror image of the respondent with that of a **responsible pro-active actor**. Such action, however, requires us to assume responsibility for shaping our future with the aim of becoming **"fit for the future"** (trends and forecasts are possible aids without overestimating them). This puts us in a position not only to make small improvements, but also to generate the great innovations that are associated with a necessary change in our behavior and can thus pave the way for truly sustainable development. Social, ecological and economic development aspects combine to form a synergetic whole.

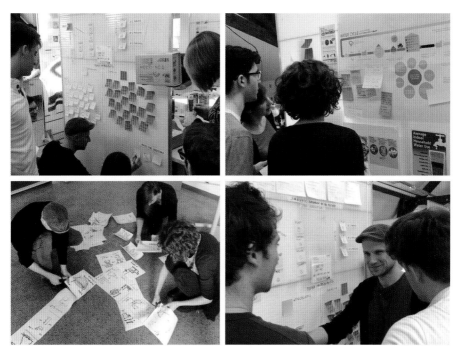

Students at the workshop as part of the project "Future of the bath" with Gerald Steiner

If we now go one step further and try to understand the implications of change in relation to individual areas of life, it becomes apparent that these are always to be seen in the elementary interplay. Outstanding areas that are in a state of flux include technological developments, economic development trends, environmental and resource perspectives, social and cultural trends, demographic developments and geopolitical and regulatory trends.

When dealing with an unprecedented complexity and dynamic, the following aspects seem to have a special role to play in summary, which, however, are not to be understood separately from each other, but in an *orchestral interplay:*

Problem orientation and discovery instead of symptom treatment

Comprehensive innovative solutions require a strong problem orientation based on a pronounced understanding of the system in the future. In contrast, product orientation alone allows only segmental developments without taking into account the implications for the overall system. Likewise, especially with most complex systems today, problems are not to be understood as something given. The actual problems must often first be discovered in order to avoid symptomatic solutions and instead generate holistic ones.

System thinking in connection with integrated multidimensional sensory perceptions

Disciplinary excellence alone is rare enough. However, if it is based on the ability to recognize and understand the holistic picture, i.e., the comprehensive system with the interaction of its elements and in interaction with its environment, then an essential basis for the generation of resounding innovations, the so-called *breakthrough innovations and sustainable system innovations,* is given. This makes a completely new kind of holistic system analysis possible, which also extends to the product experience, in that products are coupled with the users through feedback mechanisms (through haptic, but also increasingly mental feedback – the latter neuronal technologies opens an undreamt-of field of action) and adapts itself accordingly self-organized. The intensive use of *different sensory perceptions* is of great importance. These include verbal and visual approaches and representations, extended by auditory, kinesthetic or haptic, olfactory, but also gustatory sensory impressions, which are additionally extended by mental simulations and emotionality. Design-based problem-solving methods increasingly demand integrated, *multidimensional sensory perceptions* and *emotionality* in the sense of an interface function within the framework of knowledge integration (e.g., between disciplines, stakeholder groups, analytical thought processes and creative processes, between cognition and emotion, between different subsystems such as coupled human-environment systems), but also in a new *sensuality of products* as an overall experience that can be experienced through different sensory perceptions.

Human-centered design in the age of digitization

Today, design processes are predominantly embedded in coupled human-environment systems. Consequently, the human being (whether as user, non-user, person affected, etc.) is at the center of the understanding and the development process based on it. In other words: "System understanding and stakeholder analysis followed by scenario development and the generation of products and processes as means of intervention." Understanding the *interaction of the physical and digital worlds* is essential to assess the future impact of system interventions in the form of innovation and their feedback mechanisms.

The reduction and the exclusive trust in the digital world could not only result in a lack of understanding, but could also ultimately become a danger to humanity in the sense of Orson Welles.

Increasing importance of collaborative forms of work and participative designs
Increasing networking and complexity require the interaction of a wide variety of perspectives from different disciplines and actors. The focus here is on joint development: whether technological, product, service or social developments, comprehensive system innovation or the development of entrepreneurial and political programs; *collaborative procedures* in the form of interdisciplinary teams of experts involving a wide range of social actors are becoming a success factor for sustainable innovation developments. Although the will is an essential prerequisite for successful implementation, it also requires the corresponding *personal, sociocultural, creative, professional and systemic skills.* However, it is essential, in the sense of the given role profile and its competencies, to also assume responsibility for one's own area of expertise with regard to *transdisciplinarity* (being an expert in a specific area also means taking responsibility for this area). Furthermore, in the sense of participative design, the project phases in which the involvement of lead users, users, other stakeholders and other experts and representatives of society appear to make sense must be precisely defined.

Process-oriented creativity
Uncertainty regarding future developments requires not only convergent thinking, based on structured logical-rational process orientation, but also divergent thinking, i.e., the ability to find new solutions through free associations. Through the synergy of divergent and convergent thinking, a process-oriented form of creativity becomes possible. While individual creative achievements have been characteristic for a long time, today and in the future it is increasingly collaborative creative achievements that are the driving force for the development of sustainable innovations.

Resilience and sustainable development as meta goals in the design process
Current and past social developments prove that design should increasingly devote itself to a higher task. These are the strengths in connection with multidimensional knowledge integration which are of central importance not only for new products and processes, but for holistic system innovations as an intervention in the sense of society's ability to survive and thus its resilience and sustainability.

Where will design develop as a discipline?
Two extreme positions are mentioned here, whereby the real manifestations are somewhere in the field of tension between design as a tool and design as a comprehensive development approach: on the one hand, design as a tool in the service of a consumer society with the aim of making products and services more attractive, more esthetic, more fashionable, easier to use and more marketable. On the other hand, design as a comprehensive development approach which can contribute to a better understanding of the complex world and its cultural and contextual realities. This should ensure an integrated system development which is of far-reaching importance. For Tim Brown, for example, CEO of the design company IDEO, design should generate solutions for today's major challenges, such as global warming, education, health, safety, water supply, etc. Comprehensive system considerations and problem-solving processes in synthesis between cognition and emotion are essential prerequisites for design processes.

If design actually strives for integrated system developments and significant innovations, this is not only associated with amenities and an openness to change. Rather, change also means overcoming immanent inertia and habits and sometimes even abandoning the old in order to generate something new based on it. The Austrian national economist J.A. Schumpeter also described this effect as "creative destruction" and thus pointed out a characteristic that is or will be influential then as well as now and for all future developments. The greater the change brought about, the greater the uncertainty of its effect and consequently the greater the tendency of those who have benefited from previous solutions to persist. Innovations that do not take this into account can be quickly pulverized despite far-reaching potential for improvement.

A key factor for successful future design developments is not only to follow a certain development path. Instead, it will become increasingly important to derive potential future scenarios based on a profound systemic understanding of current influencing variables and to generate creative developments that are not only of economic importance, but also visionary and significant for truly sustainable development.

Gerald Steiner

Professor Dr. Gerald Steiner is Dean of the Faculty of Economics and Globalization at the Danube University Krems and since 2015 Professor of Organizational Communication and Innovation. From 2011 to 2015 he was a Schumpeter Fellowship Professor at Harvard University and visiting scholar. Before his professional career led him to the USA, he habilitated in the Department of Systems Management and Sustainability Management at the University of Graz in 2009 and represented this department as Associate Professor at the Institute for Systems Sciences, Innovation and Sustainability Research, for which he was jointly responsible in 2007.
As a lecturer in the field of innovation management and systemic-creative problem-solving methods at the Industrial Design course at FH JOANNEUM in Graz, he supports students in their project-specific creative and innovation processes.
In addition to his academic career, he was responsible for product innovations for a wide variety of companies in the field of special mechanical engineering, as well as for system innovations, primarily due to his independent business activities.
His book "Das Planetenmodell der kollaborativen Kreativität: Systemisch-kreatives Problemlösen für komplexe Herausforderungen" (The Planetary Model of Collaborative Creativity: Systemic-Creative Problem Solving for Complex Challenges), was published in 2011 by Gabler-Research and is of great relevance regarding today's major social challenges. This was followed by numerous international journal publications, including the Harvard Publication Series.

Index design

Appendix

EXPLANATION OF TERMS

Appearance = that part of the product quality which consciously or unconsciously triggers a positive, sensual effect in the viewer of a product.

Indicator function = term from product semantics: the design provides direct indications of the practical function by means of a corresponding symbolism.

Esthetics = the study of appearances that can be perceived with the senses and human perception. It not only includes visual impressions, but also acoustic, haptic ones, etc.

Animation (used here to mean computer animation) = camera shots or a film of sequences of movements of design objects that do not yet exist using computer models.

Anthropometry = the study of human body measurements and ratios of measurements. Important complementary science for ergonomics.

Brainstorming = systematic method of generating ideas. Carried out in groups according to certain rules (e.g., no killer phrases, visualizing, etc.).

Briefing = design briefing = a concise description or list of all the factors, requirements and requests affecting product design. Can also be taken to mean a design-specific shortened form of the specifications.

CAD = Computer Aided Design of a product = modeling various features of a product.

CAID = Computer Aided Industrial Design = systems tailored to industrial designers' needs, such as designing complex freeform surfaces.

CAM = Computer Aided Manufacturing = computer numeric control (CNC) with CAD data is used for machines to achieve greater precision and efficiency.

Clay modeling = common technique primarily used in transportation design. Clay is industrial plasticine that becomes soft enough when heated to around 50 degrees to be applied to a rigid foam core. The required shape is obtained by removing some of the clay with a scraper, templates, etc.

Corporate design = the creation of a company's image (corporate identity), which also requires a suitable corporate philosophy.

Corporate identity = a company's image, which not only applies outwardly to the customers, but also inwardly to the employees. It ranges from notepaper to products and architecture.

Design = detailed planning in the sense of a comprehensive problem-solving process. It can refer to services, products, vehicles, systems, etc. Used in this book as an abbreviation for industrial design (see below).

Design model = model that is a true representation of the product's future look – without being functional. Task for professional modelers (also called presentation model, see also mock-up).

Design study = design project of a visionary character – very often used for presenting new ideas. However, it can also be further optimized for reaching the production stage.

Dimension drawings = views produced with line drawings showing the most important measurements for building a development.

Ecology = the study of the relationships and interactions between living organisms and between organisms and their environment.

Ergonomics = the study of adapting the workplace – and therefore products – to people. Especially important, e.g., when designing displays and controls (also called human engineering).

Ergonomic model = model for checking ergonomic qualities, such as handling, sitting position, vision conditions, etc.

Exploded view = method of showing complex product structures more clearly as separate components but with their relative positions maintained.

Face-lifting = smartening up of a product that appears outdated. Unlike redesign, face-lifting is restricted to the product language qualities and does not include the practical function.

Freedom of form = the creative freedom that remains after fundamental values, target group relationships and similar restrictions are taken into consideration.

Function model = model for checking a technical function (mechanical or electronic), irrespective of design.

Utility value = identical with product quality. Used in the past mostly only in the sense of practical or technical function, today extended to the esthetic and symbolic use of products.

Haptic = relating to the sense of touch with the whole hand, e.g., when taking hold of a handle, knob, etc. (not to be confused with "tactile").

Industrial design = detailed planning of products or systems to be manufactured industrially. Industrial design is a holistic problem-solving process with the aim of adapting consumer goods to the user's needs, and also meeting the demands of the market, corporate identity and economic manufacture in the company's interests. In addition, it is a cultural, social and ecological factor.

Interface design = the design of the interfaces from analog to digital content. It is about the concrete visible design on the monitor, display or touch screen, about switching or operating elements, the user interfaces of hardware or software.

Interdisciplinary work = modern, interdisciplinary work in a team – in contrast to traditional lone warfare.

Specifications = a list of all requirements related to the product, including a description of functions, performance, target group, quantities, deadlines, etc. – an important prerequisite for any product development.

Look = an appearance, style or fashion superficially reflecting the spirit of the times.

Mock-up = a non-functional, full-scale design model. The term was originally used in aviation to mean a full-sized model not capable of flying.

Mood board = sometimes also called an image board, it is a collage of pictures produced for capturing a target group's mood. What are they like? What do they read? What do they wear? How do they spend their leisure time? What products do they buy? Important for developing a target group-oriented product language.

Sustainability = a term that originates from forestry: above all, sustainable means not harvesting more than grows back. The care and use of forests must maintain their biological diversity, productivity and regenerative capacity in the long term so that these functions can be fulfilled in the future.

Sustainable design = design that contributes to higher ecological, social and economic sustainability.

Sustainable development (according to UN) = development that satisfies the needs of today's world population without compromising the opportunities of future generations.

Pilot lot sample = the first sample made with a new manufacturing tool. Used for testing or remedying faults before the start of production.

Ecology = the science that explores interactions between living beings and between them and their environment.

Package drawing = in automotive design: representation on which the most important assemblies (e.g., engine, tank, chassis) as well as the vehicle occupants are schematically represented. Starting point for a tape rendering (see there).

Specifications = a list of all requirements relating to the product, including a description of functions, performance, target group, quantities, deadlines, etc. – an important prerequisite for any product development.

Pragmatism = the relationship between signs and their users ("use").

Product analysis = method of checking a product's properties in relation to the user's requirements (expectations).

Product design = detailed planning of consumer and capital goods. Important area of industrial design (see above), but also used to distinguish it from other design disciplines, such as fashion design, transportation design, etc.

Product design = detailed planning of consumer and capital goods. Important area of industrial design (see above), but also used to distinguish it from other design disciplines, such as fashion design, transportation design, etc.

Product language = design theory developed at the University of Art and Design in Offenbach: design is taken to mean a communication medium in the sense of a "language". The "grammar" corresponds to the esthetic function, while the "content" is primarily the symbolic function.

Product quality = the effect that is produced by all the properties and features of a product to make it suitable for a certain purpose. The more it corresponds to the consumer's expectations, the higher the product quality will be considered.

Proportional model = model for checking size and proportions, usually made of easily workable materials, such as rigid foam, wood or cardboard (also called preliminary or working model).

Prototype = predominantly handmade sample of a new development, which already corresponds in form, function and material to the later serial sample as far as possible. Essential for practical testing and therefore for optimizing production documents.

Rapid prototyping = fast, cost-effective method of producing fully functional samples without having to make expensive tools. Important for the quickest possible testing and optimization with regard to series production.

Redesign = creative reworking of an existing product with the aim of increasing its utility value or updating it – from practical functions to product language aspects.

Rendering = graphic method of representation that appears three-dimensional. Drawn by hand usually using felt pens, pastel chalks and colored pencils. In CAD and CAID: photorealistic quality is achieved by covering volume or mesh models with various surfaces, colors and materials.

Scribble = hastily produced freehand sketch.

Semantics = the study of symbol functions. Products act as vehicles for meaning ("content").

Semiotics = the theory and study of signs.

Simulation = here in the sense of computer simulation: realistic representation of functional processes or their virtual testing – without a real existing model.

Sketch = English term for manually produced rendering sketches. Especially important in the concept phase of transportation design.

Stereo lithography = fully automated, computer-aided model building technology. Using laser technology, the most complex plastic parts are manufactured in a short time.

Structural model = shows the load-bearing, constructively effective structure of a concept as proof of strength, safety or manufacturability.

Styling = product cosmetics reduced to the surface. The practical functions take a back seat to the formal aspects. Styling has a one-sided show character. In colloquial language, styling is often mistakenly equated with design.

Symbol function = term from product semantics: the design provides indirect references to sociocultural backgrounds through its corresponding symbolic character. It can also be understood as an "owner level".

Syntactics = the study of the relationship between characters ("grammar/form").

Tactile = perception through touch with the fingertips. Important when designing surface structures, edges and radii (not to be confused with "haptic").

Tape rendering = a technique mainly used in transportation design. Using tapes (self-adhesive tapes in various widths), vehicle contours, light edges, etc. are displayed on translucent plastic films. The advantage over markers is that all lines can be corrected at any time.

Usability = the usability of products and systems. The term usability originally comes from ergonomics and was used to analyze the human-machine interface. Today, usability has an extended spectrum of meaning and describes all interactions between people (users) and their designed environment. It includes products, user interfaces (screen/touch screen), but also services and experiences.

User interface design (UI) = in the field of electronics the planning of the human-machine interface, especially taking the finding in ergonomics and perception psychology into consideration.

User experience (UX) = describes the perceptions and reactions of people when using a product, i.e., the user experience. This refers to the user's emotions, psychological and physiological reactions, and expectations when dealing with the product.

Value analysis = a holistically effective and function-oriented, systematic method of examination, which enables opportunities to be developed for producing the value of a product or service expected by the customer at the lowest possible cost or achieving (functional) value added for the same price.

DESIGN ORGANIZATIONS / WEBSITES / LITERATURE

Design organizations:

World Design Organisation, WDO:	www.wdo.org
BEDA Bureau of European Designers' Assocations:	www.beda.org
AIGA, the professional association for design:	www.aiga.org
AGD Allianz deutscher Designer e.V./ Alliance of German Designers:	www.agd.de
Cumulus the International Association of Universities and Colleges of Art, Design and Media:	www.cumulusassociation.org
VDID Verband Deutscher Industrie Designer:	www.vdid.de
Rat für Formgebung/German Design Council:	www.german-design-council.de
Design Austria:	www.designaustria.at
Creative Industries Styria:	www.cis.at
Swiss Design Association:	www.swiss-design-association.ch

Websites:

Car design:	www.cardesignnews.com
	www.cartype.com
	www.simkom.com
Presentation techniques:	www.artbyfeng.com
	www.designstudiopress.com
	www.thegnomonworkshop.com
Design network:	www.designboom.com
	www.designsojourn.com
	www.idsa.org
	www.stylepark.com
Industrial design:	www.designaddict.com
	http://designthinking.ideo.com
	www.dezeen.com
Lifestyle/design/architecture:	www.thecoolhunter.net
	www.wired.com/gadgetlab
Materials/innovations:	www.designinsite.dk
	www.innovationlab.eastman.com
	www.materialconnexion.com
Trend analyses:	www.wgsn.com
	www.trendwatching.com

Magazines:

Auto & Design (Italy):	www.autodesignmagazine.com
AXIS Magazine (Japan):	www.axisinc.co.jp
Car Styling (Japan):	www.carstylingmag.com
design4disaster:	www.design4disaster.org
design report (Germany):	www.designreport.de
dezeen, Sustainable Design (London):	www.dezeen.com/tag/sustainable-design/
form (Germany):	www.form.de
inhabitat:	www.inhabitat.com
interiormotives (Great Britain):	www.interiormotivesmagazine.com
Intersection (Great Britain):	www.intersectionmagazine.com
New Design (Great Britain):	www.newdesignmagazine.co.uk

BOOK RECOMMENDATIONS

Design classics:

Aicher, Otl:	die welt als entwurf: schriften zum design, Ernst & Sohn, Munich, 1991
Gros, Jochen:	Grundlagen der Theorie der Produktsprache – Einführung, Offenbach, 1983
Klöcker, Ingo:	Produktgestaltung, Berlin, 1981
Loewy, Raymond:	Hässlichkeit verkauft sich schlecht, Düsseldorf, 1992
Loos, Adolf:	Ornament & Vebrechen, (ed. Peter Stuiber) Metroverlag, Vienna, 2012
Papanek, Victor:	Design for the real World, Pantheon Books, New York, 1971
Rams, Dieter:	Weniger aber besser, Jo Klatt Design+Design Verlag, Hamburg, 1995
Schürer, Arnold:	Der Einfluß produktbestimmender Faktoren auf die Gestaltung, Bielefeld, 1974
Sullivan, Louis H.:	The Tall Office Building Artistically Considered, in: Lippicott's, 1896
Winter, Friedrich G.:	Gestalten: Didaktik oder Urprinzip, Ravensburg, 1984

Design standard works:

Berents, Catharina: Kleine Geschichte des Design,
Verlag C. H. Beck, Munich, 2011

Bouroullec, Ronan/Bouroullec, Erwan: Ronan and Erwan Bouroullec,
Phaidon Press, London, 2008

Böhm, Florian: KGID: Konstantin Grcic Industrial Design,
Phaidon Press, London, 2007

Bürdek, Bernhard E.: Design: Geschichte, Theorie und Praxis der Produktgestaltung,
Birkhäuser, Cologne, 2015

Dorschel, Andreas: Gestaltung – Zur Ästhetik des Brauchbaren,
Universitätsverlag Winter, Heidelberg, 2003

Erlhoff, Michael/Marshall, Tim: Wörterbuch Design,
Birkhäuser Verlag, Basel/Boston/Berlin, 2008

Eisele, Petra: Klassiker des Produktdesign, Reklam, Munich, 2014

Eissen, Koos/Steur, Roselien: Sketching 5th Print: Drawing Techniques for Product Designers,
Bis Publishers, Amsterdam, 2007

Fuad-Luke, Alastair: The Eco-design Handbook, Thames & Hudson, London, 2009

Hauffe, Thomas: Geschichte des Designs, DuMont Buchverlag, Cologne, 2014

Krippendorff, Klaus: Die semantische Wende: Eine neue Grundlage für Design,
Birkhäuser, Basel, 2012

Morrison, Jasper: Everything but the Walls, Baden, 2006

Nachtigall, Werner/Blüchel, Kurt G.: Das große Buch der Bionik, DVA Verlag, Stuttgart 2003

Papanek, Victor: The Green Imperative: Ecology and Ethics in Design and Architecture,
Thames & Hudson, London, 1995

Polster, Bernd: Braun: 50 Jahre Produktinnovationen,
DuMont Buchverlag, Cologne, 2005

Stebbing, Peter/Tischner, Ursula: Changing Paradigms: Designing for a Sustainable Future,
Cumulus Association (ed.), Aalto University Helsinki, 2015,
http://www.cumulusassociation.org/changing-paradigms-designing-for-a-sustainable-future/

Steffen, Dagmar (ed.): Design als Produktsprache: Der Offenbacher Ansatz in Theorie und Praxis,
with contributions by Bernhard E. Bürdek, Volker Fischer, Jochen Gros,
Verlag form theorie, Frankfurt am Main, 2000

Selle, Gert: Geschichte des Design in Deutschland,
Campus Verlag, Frankfurt am Main, 2007

Tedesch, Arturo: AAD Algorithms-Aided-Design,
Le Penseur Publisher, Brienza, 2014

Tischner, Ursula et al.: Was ist EcoDesign?, Umweltbundesamt (ed.), 2015,
https://itunes.apple.com/de/book/was-ist-ecodesign/id1124326456?mt=11

Tilley, Alvin R.: The Measure of Man and Woman: Human Factors in Design,
Henry Dreyfuss Associates, Berlin, 2002

Welzer, Harald/Sommer, Bernd: Transformationsdesign — Wege in eine zukunftsfähige Moderne,
oekom Verlag, Frankfurt, 2014

PICTURE CREDITS

BACHELOR/MASTER DEGREE PROGRAM

Bachelor of Arts in Arts and Design/B.A.
6 semesters/180 ECTS (full-time)/18 places per year
www.fh-joanneum.at/industrial-design/bachelor/

Master of Arts in Arts and Design/M.A.
4 semesters/120 ECTS (full-time)/18 places per year
www.fh-joanneum.at/industrial-design/master/

Institute of Product & Transportation Design of the
FH JOANNEUM University of Applied Sciences
Alte Poststraße 149, 8020 Graz, Austria
Tel: +43(0)316-5453-8100/E-mail: ide@fh-joanneum.at

f facebook FH JOANNEUM Industrial Design
vimeo https://vimeo.com/user63132342
Linked in FH JOANNEUM Industrial Design Linked in

 Information
about studies

 VIMEO video portal of
FH JOANNEUM Industrial Design

We wish to thank the students, graduates and companies for their kind support.

Published with the kind support of Accenture.